WHO TOLD YOU
THAT YOU WERE NAKED?

A Refreshing Reexamination of the Garden of Eden

By William E. Combs

Carpenter's Son Publishing

Published by Carpenter's Son Publishing,
Franklin, Tennessee

Published in association with
Larry Carpenter of Christian Book Services, LLC
www.christianbookservices.com

Cover and Interior Design by William E. Combs
Public Domain Cover Photo by 'Bobbi Jones' Jones
Edited by Robert Irvin
Printed in the United States of America
978-1-942587-68-2

Table of Contents

To Miriam in loving memory,
   my God-given soul mate,
      my wife for forty-eight wonderful years,
         filled with love, courage, strength, and wisdom.

You were my warm, golden Sunrise,
   my deep and abiding Joy,
      my Bride, my Song,
         my Treasure, my closest Friend.

Oh, to see your clear blue eyes,
   and hear your joy-filled laughter ring!
      All these things I've said and more,
         convince me that you're blessed by God.

Special thanks to family and friends for supporting me with their encouragement and prayers while I was developing this manuscript from a sermon idea to its present form:

Valerie Saunders, Ron Combs, Mike and Cheryl Combs, John and Linda Combs, Lana Combs, Edie Johnson, Ralph and Betty Thomas, Al and Sharon Royce, Wayne and Suzanne Bowen, Louine Verneuil, Kerry and Jackie Schmidt, Marty and Barb Ferguson, Al and Lola Cain, Jim and Luella Lindley, John and Peggie Gillespie, Gloria Irwin, Mark and Ginny Bigelow, Scotty and JoAnne Cookston, Jim and Christie Garras, Linda Anderson, Russ and Louise Simmelink, Bill Davenport, Keith and Nancy Arnold, Fred and Ardi Lupton, Larry and Becky Bugbee, Nick and Blanche Campbell, and Jonathan and Jennifer Lucero.

Special kudos to my friends, the reverends Al and Mary DeHaven, retired missionaries to Scotland, who gave me an initial critique of the manuscript along with suggestions for study questions.

I am also indebted to Larry Carpenter, president of Carpenter's Son Publishing, and his superb staff for guiding and encouraging me at every turn through the bewildering maze of decisions and commitments to successfully publish this book; to Joni Sullivan Baker, my publicist, who often climbed to the "crow's nest" on our marketing "ship" to scout out and secure the best tactics for getting this book into the hands of prospective readers; to Bob Irvin, my professional editor, who not only brought my manuscript up to the standards of the current *Chicago Manual of Style*, but also took extra care and time to improve my writing techniques as well; and to Britni Rickson, project manager for Color House Graphics, for her invaluable print formatting insights.

Introduction

My first encounter with light as more than illumination from a flashlight was on our homestead in Alaska at age five. Our family's modern conveniences were only two: Coleman lanterns and an indoor pitcher pump.

The three-holer behind our house, however, was the envy of our neighbors. My grandpa built it even before our house was complete. He was a large, friendly man, intensely proud that we had journeyed over the Alcan highway from Phoenix to the Matanuska Valley shortly after World War II to try our hand at farming. No unisex, one-size-fits-all outhouse for his daughter's family! Only a well-designed, ergonomically engineered masterpiece providing years of trouble-free service would do.

Grandpa constructed the walls from bark-edged boards, the first cuts from logs at the mill. This lumber kept the cost of the project down and contributed to the rustic, country appearance he was after. A tar paper roof enhanced its rural ambiance and he fitted the inside of the door with a brass hook for extra privacy.

Next, he lavished his loving attention on the structure's

interior, sanding the sides and top of the furniture-grade fir throne to a smooth, satin finish. An ample book rack and toilet paper dispenser adorned each end—along with accommodations for papa bear, mama bear, and me.

As the only lefty in the family, my little aperture was located on the left side nearer the front edge and came complete with a built-in footstool so my legs wouldn't dangle over the side.

Grandpa finished the privy before we had electricity, so it had no light bulbs or heat—minor inconveniences during Alaska's long summer days. But in the dead of winter, after he had flown back to Arizona, the darkness and sub-zero weather severely limited our outside reading.

The bitter cold did not hamper my nightly treks outdoors so much as the uneasy feeling the long nights created in me. I carried a small penlight just powerful enough to brighten the path immediately in front of my feet. On most occasions, the snow reflected the moonlight and stars, but I could also make out the shadowy forms of the trees around the house. It didn't take much imagination to hear and see all manner of foreboding creatures lurking at the edge of the woods!

I remember one night, slipping out of my warm bed and

into my wool coat, knit cap, canvas mukluks, and mittens. The crisp air bit at my nose and face as I ventured out the back door. With clear sky and no moon, the stars reached right down to the cold snow. My senses soon became accustomed to the night and I was sure I could detect something crashing through the forest in the distance.

I was just a few steps from the house when large, fresh moose tracks confronted me! The night seemed to close in on my pounding heart as I reconsidered my outing. Surely the beast would not attack me in the three-holer, so I flashed my trembling light ahead of me and hurried on.

Once inside, I listened so hard for evil noises I hardly noticed the occasional glimmer filtering through the cracks in the walls. With my business finished, I pulled up my "jammies" and cautiously stepped outside into . . . a breathtaking wonderland. From out of nowhere, a spectacular display of the northern lights set the night sky ablaze.

Huge folds of colored brilliance whipped and arced across the heavens as if dancing to an unseen choreographer's directives. At times, the hues became so intense the frost crystals covering the trees and the ice diamonds in the snow sparkled with undulating shades of yellow-green, red, and purple.

This drama so illuminated the surrounding landscape that I forgot to turn on my flashlight. Gone was the fear the tracks had elicited earlier, and in its place came a beckoning to stay and participate in the dance.

I do not know how long I stood there swaying with the silent music and marveling at its majesty. Eventually, I returned to the house and answered Mom's concern for my lengthy absence.

What a difference between a wee penlight and the splendor of the aurora borealis! My trusty possession was totally predictable. It came on at my bidding and, as long as I changed the batteries, kept my immediate horizon from playing too many tricks on me. It also focused on precisely those things in which I was interested, but its paltry beam restricted the scope of my world. The trees and snow drifts did not change with the setting of the sun, but my perception of them definitely did. My artificial candle outlined more shadows than reality and left me wrestling with images I could not perceive.

> *What a difference between a wee penlight and the splendor of the aurora borealis!*

Just as a Hebrew day is defined as a period of darkness followed by a period of light, the Old Testament is sometimes viewed as a shadow of the truth revealed in the Gospels. We are tempted to skip through this extended introduction to rejoice in God's love and forgiveness in Jesus Christ.

Like stepping out into the Alaskan winter night, I have often directed my controlled beam of spiritual illumination at those early pages, hoping to better understand the God I could not see. Each time I retraced my careful footprints from the litany of creation through Malachi, I found myself longing to walk with God as Adam and Moses did. Their light was not the Sonshine of the New Testament, but an Aurora in Excelsis Deo nonetheless!

Then quite unexpectedly, a different kind of brass hook unlatched and an old wooden door slowly creaked open in my mind. I heard the words, "Who told you that you were naked?" as though I had been there on that tumultuous afternoon with our great, great, great . . . great, great grandparents.

It is said the genesis of all biblical revelation has its roots in the first book of the Bible. My own knowledge of sin, salvation, and faith had been largely shaped through the lens of the New Testament. Standing in the garden that day, as it were, brought a much deeper understanding of these critical building blocks.

I invite you to come with me on a mission to delve into the events through which sin and death entered the world (Romans 5:12). It is my hope you too will rediscover, as I did, the glorious Light and Life available to us who believe.

In chapter one, we will visit our first parents in their new digs east of Eden, and in chapter two, we'll reexamine the circumstances that forced them to leave this idyllic lifestyle. In the third chapter, we will investigate how the devastating consequences of their actions adversely impacted both Cain and Abel and subsequently enslaved us all. Chapter four explains why I felt a reexamination of Eden was necessary.

Next, in chapter five, we begin the journey from the hopelessness of our plight as Adam's progeny to God's redemptive solution through faith in Jesus Christ. We will first examine faith itself and, in chapter six, how faith sets us free from a life of sin and death. Faith is not a one-time act but a continual walk, as we will highlight in chapter seven.

In the eighth chapter, our walk with Christ will be met with opposition from our adversary, the devil. And, despite everything the world can throw at us, chapter nine explains how we can rest in the finished work of Christ. Finally, in chapter ten, Jesus Christ calls us to deny our selves, take up our cross, and follow Him.

Oh, one more thing—for this adventure, you will not need a flashlight!

Who Told You That You Were Naked?

One
Innocent in the Garden

Adam stooped down, picked up a flat pebble, and tossed it playfully at a tuft of reeds just out from the river bank. The sound of the soft splash was quickly swallowed up in the turbulence of the river (which in time would be named the Euphrates), but still it captured his imagination. Upstream, a sea eagle descended from a giant cedar and glided silently over the shallows, its eyes riveted on a small ripple. At the last instant, its talons stretched forward and spanked the water, tearing a mangar carp from the surface. The eagle's head bobbed momentarily as it rotated its prey toward its tail and cupped the air with its majestic wings to offset the sudden acquisition. At the sight of the eagle, a pair of eider ducks exploded off the water and swiftly disappeared into the tall grass downstream.

Wading out to a sandbar, Adam climbed a rock shelf, knelt down, and peered into a limpid pool. The morning sun of late spring warmed his back as he gazed contentedly into his reflection. Had it been only a few days—maybe a bit longer?—since the Lord had brought him here to introduce him to his own image? Like the face staring back at him, those incidents shimmered and danced in his memory. A cloud drifted across the sun for a moment, and the reemerging brilliance reminded him of the One who had accompanied him that first morning.

His reverie was interrupted by a slight movement in the high grass near the water's edge. A ewe emerged to drink, her stubby tail flicking nervously as she lowered her head. Her muzzle had barely touched the water when a lioness bolted from the undergrowth, grabbed the panic-stricken victim in its powerful jaws, and dragged it back into the dense foliage.

It was over in a moment. Adam strained to hear over the river for any struggle but there was now only silence. Had the lioness been stalking him? He shuddered, realizing the ewe may have sacrificed her life for his.

Slowly, Adam waded back to shore and examined the scene of the fatal encounter. Several tufts of wool, some broken and twisted branches, and a blood-stained patch of grass marked the grisly site. By hastily retracing the ewe's footprints back into the forest, he hoped to learn a little more about her. The snap of a brittle twig beneath his foot triggered an eruption of bleating frenzy as a terrified lamb burst from a nearby clump of undergrowth where it had been hiding.

The ewe must have hidden it, Adam thought as he raced headlong after the retreating figure. The desperate creature darted into a thicket and became hopelessly entangled in the brambles. Seizing it before it freed itself and avoiding its flailing hooves, he hoisted it to his shoulders.

"I won't harm you, little one," Adam spoke reassuringly as he strode from the woods toward his home. He could feel its pounding heart, its rapid breathing, its churning efforts to escape. Gradually, however, his steady footfalls and comforting voice quieted his new friend.

Once home, he barricaded the lamb in a nook

inside his cave and constructed a stone enclosure near where he slept to watch it at night. Afterward, Adam mixed an einkorn wheat and almond slurry in a lagenaria gourd bowl, coaxed the lamb to suckle his fingers, and lowered his hand into the mix to drink. The next morning, he was delighted to observe the lamb pronging on a little knoll in the shelter . Adam decided to call her Lively.

> *"I won't harm you, little one," Adam spoke reassuringly as he strode from the woods toward his home. He could feel its pounding heart, its rapid breathing, its churning efforts to escape.*

That afternoon, he took the lamb back to the river to show it his reflection, but Lively was not the least bit interested, and Adam realized—sadly—there would be many things he could not share with his little friend.

* * * * *

Obviously, this somewhat embellished reenactment of the first days in Adams life does not come directly from Genesis 2:4-15. As we begin our quest, my desire in presenting a few short vignettes is to help us better identify with the person portrayed in the verses that are, at least for me, so familiar that it becomes difficult to see beyond the words and phrases.

Let's continue our journey.

The Garden

During one particularly pleasant early after-noon, Adam was enjoying Lively's playful antics near their home. Colorful butterflies flitted about in the refreshing Etesian breeze amid a carpet of wildflow-ers with his pet trying to chase all of them at once, much to his delight. Occasionally, Adam too joined in the festivities, darting and leaping and laughing until, thoroughly out of breath, he'd collapse on the warm, soft earth. Lying on his back, Adam closed his eyes and drank in the heady fragrances around him. A cool gust of wind rustled in the nearby pistachio trees when, suddenly, he heard the sound of the Lord approaching.

"Come with Me," beckoned the Lord, "and I will show you a marvelous place I have prepared for you." Although their trek took much of the afternoon, Ad-am hardly noticed, sharing his innermost thoughts and feelings with Lively tagging along. Then, as they came over the crest of a hill and climbed a rock outcropping, an incredible sight spread out before them.

The Lord had created a botanical paradise in a verdant landscape east of Eden. At the upper end of the garden, magnificent date palms crowded the banks of a meandering river that flowed south into reed beds alive with scarlet dragonflies, swallowtail and plain tiger butterflies, spotted crakes, marsh warblers, herons, spoonbills, and ibis.

From the north, the Etesian winds, strongest in the summer afternoons before dying down at night, swept undulating waves across a valley floor filled with native flowers, mustard, wheat, barley, lentils, peas, vetch, and patches of broad beans, onions, and garlic. Encircling this lush bounty were groves of almond, fig, olive, and pistachio trees, grapevines, and pomegranate shrubs.

"Your new home is a special place of peace, prosperity, joy, and hope," said the Lord. "You observed as we traveled here the surrounding environs are much different, and you will need to care for this oasis so it does not revert to its former existence."

The sun was setting as they finished their tour near the northern end of the valley and stood in the middle of the garden. "Look all around you and know you are free to eat the fruit of every tree except one. You must not eat the fruit from the tree of the knowledge of good and evil," the Lord warned. "For in the day you eat of it, you shall surely die." Adam shuddered at these words, recalling the gruesome demise of Lively's mother.

* * * * *

Take a closer look at this admonition from the Lord. The Hebrew word[1] for *knowledge* is represented by concepts such as discernment, perception, and wisdom and implies that if Adam ate this fruit, he would be able to grasp the good and evil implications of the situations in which he subsequently found himself. The Lord would give Adam the task of naming the birds and wild animals later that day. In doing so, He demonstrated Adam was an intelligent and perceptive person. But as yet, Adam did not have the ability to comprehend the personal ramifications of the knowledge of good and evil.

The Hebrew term for *good* has many synonyms such as

pleasing, delightful, agreeable, delicious, sweet, savory, cheerful, pure, clean, happy, glad, joyful, prosperous, and vigorous. The synonyms for *evil* are misery, distress, injury, adversity, harm, calamity, and wrong. Including these two words in God's warning to Adam indicates he must have had an intellectual understanding of this dichotomy *before* he ate the fruit of the tree. So the knowledge he would gain later would be more experiential in nature, affecting him personally.

> But as yet, Adam did not have the ability to comprehend the personal ramifications of the knowledge of good and evil.

The concept of a day as a duration of time is defined in Genesis 1:3.

> God called the light Day, and the darkness he called Night. And there was evening and there was morning, the first day.

A day is bounded by two events: evening and morning. A new day begins with the next evening and morning cycle. The same text also defines *day* as its daytime portion. This more restrictive definition definitely does not apply to Genesis 2:17. That is, the Lord was not restricting Adam from eating this fruit only during daylight hours.

However, *day* cannot be construed to convey Adam would die someday. Its designation clearly means death would come the same day he partook of the fruit.

As for the words "you shall surely die," the original language states: "in dying, you shall die." Word repetition in Hebrew is a way of emphasizing a point. In this instance, God utilized an emphatic sentence structure to communicate the critical nature of His warning. The significance of *dying* will be the subject of closer scrutiny in the next chapter.

A Helpmate for Adam

The Lord recognized from their discussions on the way to the garden that Adam was lonely; and Lively was not capable of providing the kind of friendship he needed. Knowing no other animal would satisfy his need for companionship, God paraded a veritable menagerie before Adam so he could come to this important realization.

One by one, Adam named every bird and wild beast, and whatever moniker he chose, that was its name. Those designations were not merely "antelope," "bear," "camel," "duck" . . . or "zebra." He was able to comprehend each creature's inner qualities and how that beast related to him. At the conclusion of every encounter, his response to God was likely the same: "I am still lonely for a companion—a soul mate with whom I can share everything."

So, the Lord caused Adam to fall into a deep sleep. With a natural anesthetic in place, God removed a rib from his side and performed the world's first major reconstructive surgery: He molded the rib into a woman.

When Adam awoke in this ancient form of post-op, there stood before him the most wonderful "creature" he had ever seen.

"Eureka!!" he shouted. Gazing upon her as he had done with all the other animals, he exclaimed, "This at last is bone of my bone and flesh of my flesh! A perfect helpmate for me with whom I can share everything! This awesome beauty shall be called *woman* because she was taken out of man—and is all that I am!"

* * * * *

At this point, the author of Genesis writes two verses of commentary.

> Therefore a man shall leave his father and his mother and hold fast to his wife, and they

shall become one flesh. And the man and his
wife were both naked, and were not ashamed
(Genesis 2:24, 25).

The first verse draws a parallel between the woman built

from Adam's rib and the relationship they would later enjoy

as husband and wife. They would become one flesh again—a

measure of the level of companionship and intimacy available

for all married couples who would follow. The second verse

makes certain the reader understands both Adam and his

mate were naked and were *not* ashamed. Nakedness refers on-

ly to their physical lack of clothing. Later, it will carry a much

broader meaning.

God's Plan for the Newlyweds

The Lord took these two newlyweds on anoth-

er tour—this time sharing with them a more exten-

sive plan. "Be fruitful and multiply. As your offspring

increase, this garden will not provide sufficient sus-

tenance for everyone. Therefore, I am awarding you

all the plants bearing seed and the fruit of all the

trees in the world for food.

"Initially, you will care for and maintain this

sanctuary. The surrounding environs are much different from the tranquility here. So I am granting you the authority to *subdue* the earth—to enlarge the boundaries of this estate as your family grows.

"When I brought the creatures for you to name, you discovered that not one of them was your equal. Now, I give both of you dominion over them to extend the peace of the garden to their relationships as well. To them, I give every green plant for food, so as you fill the earth and subdue it:

> The wolf shall dwell with the lamb, and the leopard shall lie down with the young goat, and the calf and the lion and the fattened calf together; and a little child shall lead them. The cow and the bear shall graze; their young shall lie down together; and the lion shall eat straw like the ox. The nursing child shall play over the hole of the cobra, and the weaned child shall put his hand on the adder's den. They shall not hurt or destroy in all my holy mountain; for the earth shall be full of the knowledge of the Lord as the waters cover the sea."

(Isaiah would later receive these words from the Lord and inscribe them in chapter 11, verses 6-9.)

The last verse of Genesis chapter 1 reads:

> And God saw everything that he had made, and behold, it was very good. And there was evening and there was morning, the sixth day.

The word translated as *good* is the same one mentioned

earlier. But the adverb *very* falls short in relating the intent of the original language. In order to emphasize the goodness of everything God had made, the narrator selected a modifier meaning "exceedingly" or "abundantly"—a much greater superlative than the descriptor "very" would imply. This expression conveys an over-the-top kind of goodness and indicates the Lord in no way considered their nakedness as a deficiency or a source of shame. Adam and his wife were two highly intelligent, perceptive, and extremely *good* jewels in the crown of His creation.

* * * * *

Fall found the couple bustling from one region of the garden to another, harvesting all manner of grains, root vegetables, fruits, and nuts. Even though it was demanding work, every afternoon was blessed with cool breezes and enriching fellowship signaled by the sound of the Lord walking toward them.

Earlier that summer, they learned how to collect date palm leaves and long rush stalks from the marshy river bank and how to dry them in the hot sun. Soon after, they split the fronds and stems into flexible strips and wove the resulting material into mats, baskets, and ropes. Now during harvest, the couple used these implements to help them thresh, gather, and store the food they would need the rest of the year.

They spent the last few days picking baskets of einkorn wheat heads and piling them on large mats. On one particular morning, Adam busied himself rubbing the wheat in his hands to separate the grain from the chaff, then heaping everything onto a different mat to be winnowed later in the afternoon.

Meanwhile, his wife traveled toward the northern end of the garden to gather the almonds that had fallen from the trees in the previous week.

Study Questions for Discussion

- Why did God give Adam and Eve "every plant yielding seed that is on the face of all the earth, and every tree with seed in its fruit" when the Garden yielded such a bounty of food (Genesis 1:29)?

- God told them to "be fruitful and multiply and fill the earth" (Genesis 1:28). Would the garden ultimately be just a localized staging area to "work and keep" (Genesis 2:15) or a remote vacation spot or could it have been part of a larger plan for them?

- Why did God charge them to *subdue* the earth "and have dominion over the fish of the sea and over the birds of the heavens and over every living thing that moves on the earth" (Genesis 1:28)?

- God gave all the other creatures of the earth every green plant for food (Genesis 1:30). Do you see any association with Isaiah 11:6-9?

- Why did God bring all the beasts of the field and every bird of the heavens to see what Adam would call them? Is there more to naming than a taxonomical designation? See Exodus 3:13, 14; Isaiah 62:2; Revelation 2:17, 3:12.

- What was Adam indicating when he named his wife *woman* (Genesis 2:23)?

- Since Adam was intelligent and insightful enough to name all these creatures and his helpmate, what do you think was his initial understanding, as a truly innocent person, of God's warning not to eat the fruit of the tree of the knowledge of good and evil (Genesis 2:17)?

- According to Genesis 2:17, when would Adam die if he ate the fruit of the tree of the knowledge of good and evil?

Two
Naked in the Garden

The Serpent

The crafty serpent waited for just such a moment: the woman was alone in the middle of the garden, and he called to her as she passed near the tree of the knowledge of good and evil.

"Did the Lord say you couldn't eat from any tree in the garden?" the serpent quietly asked.

"Not so," Adam's wife replied. "We may consume the fruit of all of the trees, except one." Pointing to the tree of the knowledge of good and evil, she declared, "God has only prohibited us from ingesting this fruit. In fact, He has prohibited us from even *touching* it, lest we die."

The serpent smiled reassuringly and replied, "No, my dear, you will not die. The Lord knows when you taste this fruit, your eyes will be opened and you will become like Him, knowing good and evil."

These comments had a certain ring of validity to them, for she realized there was nothing foreboding about the fruit. In fact, it seemed exceptionally attractive to her, and certainly did not appear poisonous. Since she had not been there when the Lord gave Adam this warning, *maybe he misunderstood the instructions*, she reasoned. After all, the tree occupied a prominent place directly next to the tree of life. *Perhaps, this knowledge would make one wise*, she thought.

With persistent encouragement from the serpent, she cautiously stepped forward and plucked one of the low-hanging fruit.

There . . . she had done the unthinkable. Crouching down with hunched shoulders, she held her breath for what seemed like an eternity and squeezed her eyes shut, dreading what must inevitably happen next. But instead of pain shooting up her arm as she expected, sending her writhing to the ground in anguish, the fruit just sat there in her hand, delectable as ever.

Slowly she straightened up and reassessed her condition. Nothing she had feared was happening to her! Perhaps the serpent was right. Finally, with more reassurance, she bit into the fruit. Mouthwatering juice ran down her cheeks and neck, and for a moment, the sheer enjoyment of this delightfully new treat overwhelmed her senses. But as she swallowed, she once again braced for an imagined episode of torment.

There . . . she had done the unthinkable. Crouching down with hunched shoulders, she held her breath for what seemed like an eternity and squeezed her eyes shut, dreading what must inevitably happen next.

Yet, *nothing* happened . . . nothing. *The serpent was right after all!* she thought. *Adam must have misinterpreted what was shared with him! The tree must have been planted in this prominent location for us to enjoy so we could be more like the Lord we love.* She quickly picked several especially ripe samples, placed them in her basket, and hurried back to tell her husband what she discovered. The serpent followed, reveling in the moment.

Adam looked up from his hand-threshing at the sound of his wife's excited voice, happy to see her again but surprised she had returned so soon. As she approached, she reached inside her basket, removed a ripe fruit and eagerly held it out for him to see. He thought he recognized this fruit, but certainly his initial evaluation must not be correct.

"You'll never guess what I discovered!" she shouted. "This delicious fruit is from the tree of the knowledge of good and evil . . ."

Adam stared wide-eyed at his spouse, scarcely hearing the rest of her message. Had he heard her correctly when she described the specimen in her hand as "delicious?"

"Did you hear me?" she said, responding to the shocked look on her husband's face. Adam had bolted to his feet, and she was now standing right in front of him. Pointing to an approaching figure, she continued. "The serpent helped me realize you must have misinterpreted God's warning. At first, I was quite reluctant to go near the tree. But eventually, I reached out and plucked one of its fruit. And, when I was not struck down with any of the dreadful things I imagined, I hesitantly took a bite of it. Not only did it turn out to be the most delectable treat in the garden, absolutely nothing harmful happened to me —nothing—as you can see!"

Adam's head was spinning with all this information. The injunction against touching the fruit had been his idea—just a short codicil to ensure his wife would not go near the tree and inadvertently harvest its fruit by mistake. And to give it more weight, he intimated the entire warning had come from the Lord. After all, she was the love of his life and he only wanted to protect her.[1]

It would not help much, he thought, *to inform her the additional directive was his idea*—words he now wished he could take back since the lack of consequences had emboldened her to go further. She had not only touched the fruit, she consumed one herself and was now asking him to do the same.

"Adam," she said warmly, "I know you honestly believe God warned you in the gravest imaginable way to neither eat nor touch this fruit, a fact you pointed out every time we entered the middle of the garden. Your stern admonition was one of the reasons why I also avoided the tree of life, because the two trees are so close together. We never tried the fruit of that tree either, and I am sure the Lord wants us to take pleasure in it, or He would have said something.

It would not help much, *he thought,* to inform her the additional directive was his idea— *words he now wished he could take back since the lack of consequences had emboldened her to go further.*

"The serpent convinced me that, rather than dying, our eyes would be opened, making us like gods knowing good and evil. I didn't die when I held it in my hand, much less when I ate it. Isn't it likely God planted it as a convenient resource to make us wise so we can be more like the Lord we love?"

She had a point, Adam thought. All the while his wife was talking, Adam had been scrutinizing her behavior and physical appearance and nothing had changed from her usual demeanor. How could this be? . . . unless there was something truthful to the serpent's counsel. In an impulsive moment, he decided to trust his wife's analysis: reaching out, he took the fruit from her outstretched hand, closed his eyes, and began to eat.

At first, Adam thought she must be correct. The mouthwatering taste was indescribable! But as he slowly opened his eyes to meet hers, each of them struggled with a shocking new sensation. Suddenly, they felt embarrassed and naked in front of each other. Even more distressing, they were *ashamed* of their nakedness.

After a few awkward moments trying unsuccessfully to adopt a posture that would ease their newfound predicament, the couple hastily retreated to the relative darkness of their home in a cave on the western edge of the garden. On the way, they briefly stopped to gather armfuls of large fig leaves. By the time they reached their destination, a rash from the leaves' latex sap[2] covered their arms and upper torsos.

Undeterred by the almost constant itching, each selected a length of rush-stem rope and several palm-frond strips from a storage area in their cave home. Then, using the rope as a belt and the strips as thread, they sewed the fig leaves onto the belts to make loincloths. The new apparel temporarily assuaged their self-consciousness and they soon returned to winnow the wheat Adam had threshed that morning.

What Is Nakedness?

Familiarity with this ancient text can keep us from asking an obvious question: What is nakedness? Is it simply the state of being unclothed? Genesis clearly states that in the beginning of their relationship, Adam and his wife were both naked and *not ashamed* of their nakedness.

When their eyes were opened, their actions convey that they became aware of the merits of their individual differences, the most obvious being the characteristics that distinguished them as male and female. While those differences were there all along, they now compared their own uniqueness with those of the other person in light of their newly acquired understanding. In making this evaluation, each must have concluded their own differences were not as *good* as those of their spouse.

Key to this new appraisal were perceived changes in facial expressions and tone of voice exhibited by their partner. Spousal countenance and vocal tenor were now falsely interpreted as displeasure and disapproval even though the other person's conduct was ostensibly generated by their *own* new sense of inadequacy. Unfortunately, the devastating repercussions of these subjective assessments created feelings of personal embarrassment, shame, and a growing conviction their nakedness was no longer *acceptable* to the other person.

It might seem odd this crisis occurred only after Adam consumed the fruit. Why wasn't this new realization apparent to his wife earlier? Consider the situations that elicit a person's awareness of their own nakedness.

How many times have you undressed in the privacy of your own bedroom preparing to take a bath or go to sleep— and the only other creature in the room was your cat or dog? Chances are you did not feel naked in its presence because you did not project into your pet any capacity to judge you. You instinctively knew it accepted you unconditionally, clothed or otherwise. If you are a parent, these circumstances might also extend to undressing in front of your infant child.

> *It might seem odd this crisis occurred only after Adam consumed the fruit. Why wasn't this new realization apparent to his wife earlier?*

On the other hand, have you ever dreamed you found yourself in the company of other people wearing only your birthday suit? Chances are you felt embarrassed at the possibility of being caught out in public in this uncomfortable predicament. You were probably apprehensive because *your perception of their body language convinced you* the folks in your dream observed your nakedness and formed unfavorable opinions of you.

When Adam's wife approached him, she did not perceive judgmental changes in his bearing. His greeting and accepting facial expressions did not trigger any sense of rejection because he was still innocent. It was not until Adam and his wife *both* possessed the knowledge of good and evil that they began to compare their individual differences.

Adam, Where Are You?

The pair had just finished winnowing when they heard the sound of the Lord walking toward them. This time, however, instead of rushing out to meet Him, they were terrified and swiftly scurried into a nearby pistachio grove to hide themselves from His presence.

When the Lord reached the baskets of winnowed wheat, He called out, "Adam, where are you?"

After a few agonizing moments, Adam sheepishly emerged—scratching nervously—his head bowed. His wife followed tentatively behind.

"I heard the s-sound of you w-w-walking in the garden and I was a-a-a-afraid because I was n-n-n-n-naked . . . and I hid myself," he stammered nearly uncontrollably.

"Who told you that you were naked? Have you eaten the fruit of the tree I commanded you not to eat?" the Lord asked.

"The woman whom you gave to be with me—she offered it to me and I ate it," Adam blurted, defensively.

Turning to the woman, God asked, "What is this that you have done?"

"The serpent beguiled me," she shot back, glaring at her husband—and at the serpent, who even now was trying to retreat.

* * * * *

This exchange holds several key insights into the calamitous transformation gripping the couple. Here is the world's first utterance of the word *fear*. Adam's response indicates he was not fearful he might be punished for his disobedience. He was afraid because *he felt naked.*

Unfortunately, their new fig leaf aprons did nothing to alleviate their apprehension. Until now, those garments had been sufficient to mask their embarrassment when comparing personal differences. Now, with their *eyes opened*, they made a similar mental comparison between themselves and the Lord. This time, they were overwhelmed with the conviction their own uniqueness couldn't possibly measure up to the qualities of the One who came to visit them. God also possessed this knowledge, and He must undoubtedly be displeased with their nakedness!

> *Here is the world's first utterance of the word fear. Adam's response indicates he was not fearful he might be punished for his disobedience. He was afraid because he felt naked.*

But the Lord did not disapprove. These two were the crowning achievement of His creation. Starting the question with "Who told you . . ." encouraged Adam to realize it was *not* the Lord who was judging him. Indeed, Adam's own comprehension of their relationship had precipitated *his* fearful reaction, and the only way his debilitating sense of nakedness and shame could have occurred was if he ingested the forbidden fruit.

Although Adam admitted he ate the fruit, he asserted he acted because the woman God gave him had urged him to do so. By accusing his wife—and also portraying the Lord as partially culpable—he revealed just how threatened and insecure he was and how much his opinion of the Lord's motives had changed. In Adam's eyes, God's intentions were no longer those of a person who could be trusted and who loved him and sought to restore his self-image.

Adam's wife must have felt betrayed by her husband's stinging incrimination. The Lord knew Adam's attempt to keep her from touching the fruit had unwittingly set her up to be tricked by the serpent. So, His question to her could not have been an accusation either. Sadly, her grasp of His query was also filtered, colored by her perception of His true motivation.

> *Adam's wife must have felt betrayed by her husband's stinging incrimination.*

Two Observations

The Lord's question to Adam, "*Who* told you that you were naked?" asked him to identify the person—*himself*—who was the source of his feelings of nakedness. His query to Adam's wife, "*What* is this that you have done?" focused on her *act* of eating the fruit.

In the Day You Eat of It

A barrier of mistrust was now firmly in place separating Adam and his wife from each other and from the One who wanted to redeem this situation. When the woman tried to shift the blame from herself, God turned to address the serpent.

> The Lord God said to the serpent, "Because you have done this, cursed are you above all cattle, and above all wild animals; upon your belly you shall go, and dust you shall eat all the days of your life" (Genesis 3:14).

The serpent was more than your garden variety reptile content to plunder unprotected bird nests of their eggs and nestlings. It wanted to rob Adam and his wife of their innocence. This snake was obviously an instrument of Satan, the adversary revealed in the first two chapters of the book of Job.

God did not ask any questions and there was no attempt at reconciliation or redemption. His pronouncement was intended to build a wall of enmity between the woman and the serpent so it could never again be used as a vehicle of deception. Rather than relating from a more erect stance as when it beguiled Adam's wife, it would now be sentenced to life on the ground. No longer could it communicate from a standing position, forcing its unsuspecting victim to look up when addressed. The snake would henceforth assume the lowest possible posture.

The last sentence to the serpent is directed both at the serpent and to the one who enabled the serpent to speak.[3]

> I will put enmity between you and the woman, and between your offspring and her offspring; he shall bruise your head, and you shall bruise his heel (Genesis 3:15).

The first pronoun in the second half of this sentence can be translated as "he," "she," "it," or "they" depending on the context. Since the frame of reference is not clear, this word can either be interpreted as "he" to refer to a particular male offspring[4] or as "they" to represent the woman's progeny in a more generic way. Thus, the last phrase can also be rendered: "they shall bruise your head and you shall bruise their heel."[5]

The English Standard Version (ESV) translation focuses on an ultimate victory between one of the woman's descendants and the serpent. Perhaps the pair thought Cain would fulfill this role as indicated by the way they named him at birth.

Next, the Lord spoke to Adam and his wife.

> To the woman he said, "I will surely multiply your pain in childbearing; in pain you shall bring forth children. Your desire shall be for

your husband, and he shall rule over you."

And to Adam he said, "Because you have listened to the voice of your wife and have eaten of the tree of which I commanded you, 'You shall not eat of it,' cursed is the ground because of you; in pain you shall eat of it all the days of your life; thorns and thistles it shall bring forth for you; and you shall eat the plants of the field. By the sweat of your face you shall eat bread, till you return to the ground, for out of it you were taken; for you are dust, and to dust you shall return" (Genesis 3:16-19).

Since God's words to them followed His condemnation of the serpent, one might assume He was also punishing them. After all, the second portion of the last verse seems to fulfill His warning that Adam would die: "for you are dust, and to dust you shall return." This declaration describes a person's physical death.

However, this statement cannot refer to the consequences of disobeying the Lord's command because that warning emphatically stated: "in the day that you eat of it you shall surely die." God's pronouncement to Adam and his wife only indicated they would "return to the ground" at some future date.

So, what kind of death did they incur that day? Instead of viewing death as the cessation of life, it might more appropriately be viewed as separation or alienation. In that light, *physical death* takes place when our spirit separates from our body and our body "returns to the ground."

Relational death occurs when the insecurities and self-deprecation brought on by an inner sense of nakedness alienates the participants from each other by replacing trust, compassion, unconditional love, and acceptance with suspicion and a shattered self-worth.

Spiritual death occurs when we are separated from the Lord. Adam and his wife did indeed experience relational and spiritual death that fateful day, and this alienated them from each other and from the Lord.

Even though physical death might be construed as punishment, there is another plausible explanation. During Noah's lifetime, the earth was corrupt and filled with violence. A verse from Genesis chapter 6 sheds light on how physical death in this segment should be viewed.

> Then the Lord said, "My Spirit shall not abide in man forever, for he is flesh: his days shall be 120 years" (Genesis 6:3).

Even though physical death might be construed as punishment, there is another plausible explanation.

Abide can also be translated as "contend with" (notes in the ESV) or "strive with" (King James edition). Its origins are defined by such phrases as "move in a circle," "go about," and "surround." According to Galatians 5:22, 23, the fruit of the Spirit is love, joy, peace, patience, kindness, goodness, faithfulness, gentleness, and self-control—character traits that help to countermand the destructive patterns of relational death.

Since God's Spirit abided in and surrounded Adam's progeny, contending and striving with them to postpone their demise for hundreds of years, it is unlikely physical death should be understood as punishment. More realistically, it is the consequence of several factors,[6] chief among them the devastating stresses incurred by the various aspects of relational death.

Nor should the rest of God's injunctions be viewed as punitive. As miserable and sometimes life-threatening as childbirth can be, it can create a strong sense of accomplishment and bonding with the child, bolstering the mother's self-esteem with the knowledge that her suffering brought a precious person into the world. Childbirth can also draw her husband closer to her in appreciation of what she has endured to bear their children.

Desire can also be translated as "longing." It was a good thing the Lord increased the woman's natural affection for her husband who, moments before, had accused her of causing his transgression. And because of divergent expectations, miscommunication, and differing sensitivities, this episode would not be the only time they would be at cross purposes with one another. By increasing her devotion toward Adam, God enabled her to forgive him and restore a degree of intimacy that might not otherwise have been plausible.

Rule does not mean Adam could force his wife to do his bidding. His dominion was meant to provide a loving and supportive umbrella of protection, security, and sanctity[7] as exemplified by the following New Testament passage.

> Wives, submit to your own husbands, as to the Lord. For the husband is the head of the wife <u>even as</u> Christ is the head of the church, his body, and <u>is himself its Savior</u>. Now as the church submits to Christ, so also wives should submit in everything to their husbands. Husbands, love your wives, <u>as Christ loved the church and gave himself up for her</u>, that he might sanctify her, having cleansed her by the washing of water with the word, so that he might present the church to himself in splendor, without spot or wrinkle or any blemish. <u>In the same way</u> husbands should love their wives as their own bodies. He who loves his wife, loves himself (Ephesians 5:23–28, *emphasis mine*).

And why was it important to furnish Adam's spouse with this kind of security? Generally speaking, women seem to be more relationally sensitive than men,[8] both on interpersonal as well as spiritual levels. When the serpent chose to reveal himself to Adam's wife, he waited until she was alone and counted on her eagerness to be more like the One who came to commune with them each afternoon. By doing so, the serpent took advantage of her relational sensibilities to trick her into eating the forbidden fruit.

The Lord told Adam's mate her husband would rule over her, giving her a way to delay committing to any course of action until both agreed the decision was blessed by God. In this way, her sensitivity would be a powerful asset to their relationship, enhancing their skillfulness as a team.

> *When the serpent chose to reveal himself to Adam's wife, he waited until she was alone and counted on her eagerness to be more like the One who came to commune with them each afternoon.*

God's admonition to Adam might seem punitive, particularly since the Lord began by reminding him of his transgression. But once again, these words are *redemptive*. Just as childbearing could bolster his wife's self-respect, so too the constant challenges of laboring in the fields could give Adam a true sense of accomplishment.

Until that day, the garden yielded its bounty with few if any impediments, leaving the couple with ample spare time to enjoy the Lord and each other and to savor their spectacular environment. But now, an abundance of free time would give them more occasion to ruminate on their individual differences, compounding their feelings of insufficiency.

Instead of an abundant harvest, the land would now be choked with thorns and thistles, crowding out the plants that would be the source of their daily food. Wrestling with these problems would more than fill Adam's waking hours, at times leaving him exhausted and discouraged his labors yielded so little in comparison with the effort he expended.

But these trying circumstances would also test his resourcefulness and creativity, reinvigorating his self-worth as he overcame each trial to care for and sustain his family. His accomplishments could also strengthen their marriage, reinforcing his wife's wholesome pride in his ability to support their expanding needs.

Lamentably, the couple would be required to move from their oasis of peace, prosperity, joy, and hope—and into the surrounding environs where thorns and thistles were commonplace. Their original mission of extending the boundaries of the garden was now a fading, disappointing memory. But rather than heaping more blame on his wife, Adam gave her a new name.

> The man called his wife's name Eve, because she was the mother of all living (Genesis 3:20).

According to the notes in the English Standard Version: "*Eve* sounds like the Hebrew for *life-giver* and resembles the word for *living*." He had named his pet Lively to denote her playful spirit. And now, instead of looking back to all the turmoil of the day, Adam looked ahead, viewing his wife with new admiration and respect. He lovingly called her Eve because she would be the mother of all their descendants.

Better Garments

Then God gave them better garments to cover their nakedness.

> And the Lord God made for Adam and his wife garments of skins and clothed them (Genesis 3:21).

Understandably, the couple was quite reluctant to leave their home. So when they tarried, God drove them out for their own sake.

The goal of redeeming creation would now include Adam, Eve, and their offspring and would be carried out by another Adam.[9]

And raiment made by the Lord for them from the skins

of animals would also be replaced in the future when God would clothe all believers in His righteousness through the ultimate sacrifice of His Son.

Study Questions for Discussion

- Was the crafty serpent an instrument of Satan or Satan himself posing as a serpent?

  - How does Genesis 3:14 fit in with your decision?

- Where do you think Adam's wife got the phrase "neither shall you touch it" (Genesis 3:3)?

- She saw that "the tree was good for food, and that it was a delight to the eyes, and that the tree was to be desired to make one wise" (Genesis 3:6). How do you interpret this verse in light of the fact that she was a truly innocent person and not as yet "in the world" (1 John 2:16-17)?

  - Since she was deceived by the serpent, how do you interpret her desire to eat the fruit to make her wise (Genesis 3:13; 1 Timothy 2:14)?

- Is there any significance to the words *Who* and *What* in God's two queries to Adam and his wife in Genesis 3:11-13?

- What is your definition of *nakedness*?

  - When you have felt naked, was it because you were guilty?

- Why would Adam and his wife clothe themselves as soon as their eyes were opened if their nakedness was a response of guilt (Genesis 3:7)?
- Why weren't Adam's wife's eyes opened as soon as she ate the fruit (Genesis 3:6)?
  - Since their eyes were not opened until both had eaten the fruit, does that say anything about how they *perceived* their nakedness?
- Is there an explanation other than guilt for why Adam and his wife ran and hid from the Lord when they heard the sound of God walking in the garden (Genesis 3:8)?
- Why would the author of Genesis leave it to the reader to figure out the *real reason* for Adam's fear if the real reason was guilt for having disobeyed God's warning?
  - God would have known if Adam was hiding his true reason. So why didn't the Lord ask him, "What is this that you have done?" instead of asking "Who told you that you were naked?"
- Is there an explanation other than condemnation and judgment for God's pronouncements in Genesis

3:16-19?

- If they died "in the day they ate the fruit" (Genesis 2:17), what kind of death did they die?

  - Are there different *kinds* of death?

Three
Sin: Crouching at the Door

According to the apostle Paul, sin came into the world through Adam and through sin, death (Romans 5:12–14). We might be tempted to conclude the *act* of transgressing God's command was the only contributing factor causing Adam and Eve to become "sinners." If this definition were accurate, if the root meaning of sin is to be associated with Adam's *act* of transgression, then it is reasonable to assume the Lord would have used the term when He addressed the pair in Genesis chapter 3.

Cain and Abel

However, God did not employ this word until *chapter 4* in His warning to Cain. Here is the text containing the first use of the word sin.

> Now Adam knew Eve his wife, and she con-
> ceived and bore Cain, saying, "I have gotten
> a man with the help of the Lord." And again,
> she bore his brother Abel. Now Abel was a
> keeper of sheep, and Cain a worker of the
> ground. In the course of time Cain brought to
> the Lord an offering of the fruit of the ground,
> and Abel also brought of the firstborn of his
> flock and of their fat portions. And the Lord
> had regard for Abel and his offering, but for
> Cain and his offering he had no regard. So
> Cain was very angry, and his face fell. The

Lord said to Cain, "Why are you angry, and why has your face fallen? If you do well, will you not be accepted? And if you do not do well, sin is crouching at the door. Its desire is for you, but you must rule over it." Cain spoke to Abel his brother. And when they were in the field, Cain rose up against his brother Abel and killed him (Genesis 4:1–8).

Why was Cain so angry with his brother that he killed him even after receiving this warning from the Lord? While we will never know for sure, there are clues to his conduct. First, there was no special parental recognition given at Abel's birth, only that he was Cain's brother and became a shepherd. This lack of familial commendation might indicate Cain enjoyed a more favored station in the family.

Secondly, the Lord replaced loincloths with garments made from skin, implying animals had been slain. This action may well mean God established an atoning ritual for the couple's initial transgression as well as for future offerings of expiation.[1]

> *Why was Cain so angry with his brother that he killed him even after receiving this warning from the Lord? While we will never know for sure, there are clues to his conduct.*

Third, Abel's place in the family as a keeper of sheep, together with the phrase "firstborn of his flock and of their fat portions," signifies lambs were utilized in these rites and suggests a ready supply was needed for this purpose.

* * * * *

As the firstborn son, Cain followed in his father's footsteps, working side by side cultivating the plants they would need and fighting the encroachment of the thorns and thistles.

This was grueling work[2] viewed by Cain as much more demanding and essential to the well-being of the family than Abel's responsibility, even if an occasional sacrifice provided meat and clothing. As the older brother, he had taken turns with his father tending the flock until Abel was old enough. From Cain's perspective, a shepherd's life involved long stretches of little more than watching his sheep graze and sleep—a far cry from the sweat and toil he and their father encountered working the fields.

As Abel's flock expanded, he was away from home for many hours, if not days, searching for good pasture and continuously moving the sheep to allow the grass to recover from grazing. These periods of separation added to their level of misunderstanding and mistrust since the burgeoning demands of their work gave each of them less time to appreciate the contributions of the other.

The one family status Abel could claim was that the firstborn of his sheep were the offerings instituted by God. In order for Cain to participate, he needed a lamb from Abel's flock.

Cain became increasingly persuaded the Lord would surely accept an oblation from his own labors in lieu of an animal sacrifice. After all, any offering made by his parents while they were still in the garden had been grown by them. This alternative was the subject of many heated arguments between the brothers, and their relationship became so contentious and rancorous Cain could no longer bring himself to ask for a lamb from his brother.

On the day the two sons brought their offerings to the Lord, Abel protested vigorously. But Cain had convinced himself *his way was also right*, that his sibling was only objecting to an encroachment on his turf, and he proceeded with his oblation.

Regard literally means God gazed with favor on

Abel and his offering but expressed just the opposite reaction to his brother. Cain was livid. Not only was his brother's opinion vindicated, he felt humiliated in front of everyone and his rage was evident on his face.

With his pride and esteem in tatters, he knew he could no longer live in the same family with his hated brother. He looked for the first opportunity to avenge his public degradation.

> Regard *literally means God gazed with favor on Abel and his offering but expressed just the opposite reaction to his brother. Cain was livid.*

＊ ＊ ＊ ＊ ＊

This dramatization is only an attempt to explain the conflict between these two brothers; it is simply conjecture as to what might have happened. What is clear is some catastrophic meltdown occurred in this sibling relationship, a breakdown so egregious it ended with the murder of Abel at the hands of his brother.

A Context for "Sin"

The elements of this dramatization are not essential to our understanding of sin. What is important: the *context of how* sin first entered the biblical vocabulary. There is a strong parallel in the original text between this warning and the Lord's pronouncement to Adam's wife:

Genesis 3:16	Genesis 4:7
And toward your husband	And toward you
shall be your desire	is its desire
and he	but you
shall rule over you.	must rule over it.

"Shall be your desire" was spoken to *enhance* her relationship with Adam. Later, God employed this same word structure to define the role sin played in Cain's life. Instead of functioning as an influential asset, *sin was portrayed as a powerful adversary crouching at the door*, one that desired to master Cain if he failed to master it.

By describing sin in this manner, God was not associating sin with a disobedient act even though Cain's offering violated the terms shared earlier. Rather, the Lord focused on his anger and fallen countenance and the critical need to conquer his feelings. Sin was not an errant act "crouching at the door" but Cain's *perception of his relationship with his brother* that would drive him to do much worse if he did not "rule over it." And the wellspring of this attitude emanated from the knowledge of good and evil inherited from his father, Adam.

> *Sin was not an errant act "crouching at the door" but Cain's* perception of his relationship with his brother *that would drive him to do much worse if he did not "rule over it."*

Sin as an Adversary

In Romans 7:14-25, the apostle Paul also presented sin as a formidable opponent, thwarting his own inclination to do what was right.

> For we know that the law is spiritual, but I am of the <u>flesh</u>, <u>sold under sin</u>. For I do not understand my own actions. For I do not do what I want, but I do the very thing I hate. Now if I do what I do not want, I agree with the law, that it is good. So now it is <u>no longer I who do it, but sin that dwells within me</u>. For I know that nothing good dwells in me, that is, in my flesh. For I have the desire to do what is right, <u>but not the ability to carry it out</u>. For I do not do the good I want, <u>but the evil I do not want is what I keep on doing</u>. Now if I do what I do not want, it is no longer I who do it, but sin that dwells within me. So, I find it to be a law that when I want to do right, evil lies close at hand. For I delight in the law of God, in my inner being, but I see in my members <u>another law</u> waging war against the law of my mind and <u>making me captive to the law of sin that dwells in my members</u>. Wretched man that I am! Who will deliver me from this body of death? Thanks be to God through Jesus Christ our Lord! So then, I myself serve the law of God with my mind, <u>but with my flesh I will serve the law of sin</u> (*emphasis mine*).

Paul identified this adversary as another law in his members waging war against the law of his mind, making him captive to the law of sin. *Law* is not restricted to the scriptural statutes. The apostle is using it in a more generic sense as the embodiment of a norm or behavior.

Nor is Paul speaking about his pre-Christian days. This "wretched man that I am" is God's chosen apostle to the Gentiles lamenting his current condition! He is not agonizing over one or more acts of disobedience but ongoing conduct he is *incapable of overcoming*.

This rival lifestyle is none other than the knowledge of good and evil Paul and the rest of us inherited from Adam. It is a dimension of our intellect and is so innate, so instinctual, so intuitive, so pervasive a way of responding to our everyday circumstances, it is virtually impossible to avoid.

Our propensity to rely on this understanding molds our demeanor and, once established, those tendencies can be difficult if not impossible to change even when we no longer want to live that way.

It shapes our outlook, acting as a filter for our perceptions, relationships, and experiences. It is an internal voice constantly reiterating events in our past or rehearsing future encounters so that we rarely exist in the present.

Paul calls this antagonist his *flesh*—his fallen nature[3] forcing him to serve the law of sin.

Several biblical verses focus on our natural proclivity to believe the path we choose is right and good.

> Trust in the Lord with all your heart, <u>and do not lean on your own understanding</u>. In all your ways acknowledge him, and he will make straight your paths. <u>Be not wise in your own eyes</u>; fear the Lord, and turn away from evil (Proverbs 3:5–7, *emphasis mine*).

> All we like sheep have gone astray; <u>we have turned—every one—to his own way</u>; and the Lord has laid on him the iniquity of us all (Isaiah 53:6, *emphasis mine*).

> <u>There is a way that seems right to a man</u>, but its end is the way to death (Proverbs 14:12 and 16:25, *emphasis mine*).

The Fountainhead of Our Transgressions

This mindset is the fountainhead of our transgressions and is so insidious, we can overlook its impact or even its existence and concentrate instead on remedying unwanted habits. By reducing sin to a mere list of offenses, we can convince ourselves we are becoming better persons because we are committing fewer "sins" than we once did.

This attitude shifts our focus away from the devastating consequences of sin—the inner conviction we do not measure up. We need to hear the Lord asking us, "Who told you that you need to be thinner, younger, healthier, prettier, more athletic, more intelligent, one who speaks with more confidence, have a better sense of humor, with fewer zits, a bigger home in a more upscale neighborhood, a more important job with a larger paycheck, a newer, faster, or classier car, more stylish clothing, more influential friends, or more time to devote to the things you want to do?"

We can "clothe" ourselves with the trappings of wealth, education, a notable position, or even religious piety in an attempt to persuade ourselves we no longer feel vulnerable.

Or, we can grapple with the gravity of our situation and acknowledge with Paul the "other law" in our members waging war against us and making us captive to the law of sin. This admission is not just a one-time event but a continuous, lifelong recognition of *our total inability to free ourselves* from our feelings of nakedness.

Study Questions for Discussion

- Why did God wait until Genesis chapter 4 to use the word *sin*?

  - Should we pay any attention to the context of the way a word is first used in the Bible?

  - What is the context for the word *sin* in Genesis 4:3-7?

- Why didn't Paul say "For as in Adam *and Eve* all die, so also in Christ shall all be made alive" (1 Corinthians 15:22)?

- In Romans 7:14-25, Paul says he had the desire to do what was right but not the ability to carry it out because he was captive to the law of sin dwelling in his members. What does his use of the word *law* mean?

  - Was Paul speaking as an unbeliever or as God's apostle to the Gentiles when he penned, "Wretched man that I am! Who will deliver me from this body of death" (Romans 7:24)?

  - Paul also says with his *flesh*, he will serve the law of sin (Romans 7:25). How are these terms associated with the knowledge of good and evil both he and the rest of us inherited from Adam?

- Does the law of sin refer to a list of sinful acts or to a way of life that generates specific acts of sin?

- Does the law of sin and death (Romans 8:2) relate to Proverbs 14:12 and 16:25?

- What motivated the rich young ruler to ask Jesus, "Teacher, what good deed must I do to have eternal life" (Matthew 19:16)?

  - Jesus replied: "Why do you ask me about what is good? There is only one who is good." Why did Jesus focus on the word *good* (Matthew 19:17)?

- Why does reducing sin to a list of offenses limit our ability to deal with the law of sin?

Four
Why Reexamine Eden?

Perhaps when you read the subtitle to this book, *A Refreshing Reexamination of the Garden of Eden*, you viewed it as a clever phrase designed to entice people to buy the product. Maybe you have never studied any commentaries on Genesis and don't see anything "refreshing" in the first three chapters. But if you researched Genesis, this presentation stands in stark contrast with a number of commentaries[1] that describe the third chapter of Genesis as a litany of rebellion and judgment. Here are the critical areas of contrasting opinions.

To Touch or Not to Touch

Adam's wife responded to the serpent's first question, adding an additional phrase to God's original admonition.

> "We may eat of the fruit of the trees in the garden, but God said, 'You shall not eat of the fruit of the tree in the midst of the garden, <u>neither shall you touch it</u>, lest you die'" (Genesis 3:2, 3, *emphasis mine*).

Some see in this addendum a growing resentment at the restriction placed upon her and her husband, the thought that:

We can't even touch the fruit from this tree!

It would be a challenge to pluck a specimen from the tree and consume it without holding it. Why would the Lord warn Adam not to eat the fruit but then later, in another conversation, add to that decree by forbidding the couple from even touching it? Since touching would also incur death, why not make that deed the focus of His initial command? That He did not mention handling the fruit in Genesis 2:16, 17 raises serious doubts God added it later.

Secondly, the Lord's warning began with the words, "You may surely eat from every tree in the garden." The garden offered a readily available cornucopia of fruits, nuts, seeds, and vegetables. God's injunction included *only one tree*—hardly a sufficient reason to rebel against the His authority.

People who experience a close encounter with the Lord report how loving, gracious, and caring He is.

✶ ✶ ✶ ✶ ✶

Personal Testimony

While in college, long before we were married, my wife Miriam struggled through an especially difficult week. Exhausted, she retired to her dorm room to lay down for several minutes before going to dinner at the school's cafeteria. Many students were still in class and because it was December in Alaska, her room was dark.

She had only drifted off for a few moments when a warm, soothing, glowing light surrounded her. Her only thought: *I am resting in the Everlasting Arms.* She felt completely at peace in the loving embrace of her heavenly Father and did not want to leave.

All too soon, though, she awoke in the unlit room and patted her pillow, trying to return to that moment. Her encounter only lasted a few minutes, yet she felt rested as though she had slept an entire night.

* * * * *

Since God never changes, we can assume Adam and his wife enjoyed a similar relationship with Him. It seems much more obvious the sanction not to touch the fruit came from Adam in an attempt to protect his wife than that the warning originated with God.

> *It seems much more obvious the sanction not to touch the fruit came from Adam in an attempt to protect his wife than that the warning originated with God.*

She Analyzed the Fruit

> But the serpent said to the woman, "You will not surely die. For God knows that when you eat of it your eyes will be opened, and you will be like God, knowing good and evil." So when the woman <u>saw that the tree was good for food, and that it was a delight to the eyes, and that the tree was to be desired to make one wise</u>, she took of its fruit and ate and she also gave some to her husband who was with her, and he ate (Genesis 3:4–6, *emphasis mine*).

Some see in the underlined words a parallel with 1 John 2:16.

> For all that is in the world—the desires of the flesh and the desires of the eyes and pride of life—is not from the Father but is from the world.

Notice the first phrase: "All that is in the world." Adam's wife was innocent and not as yet "in the world." Her innocent nature made her totally incapable of having desires of the *flesh* and the *pride* of life. Instead, she employed her God-given perceptive intellect to analyze the fruit before ingesting it—the same kind of analysis Adam had previously used to name all the animals.

These commentaries say the temptation to be like God, to gain the knowledge of good and evil in her own right, filled her with such desire that she ate the fruit. However, when confronted by the Lord, she said the serpent had deceived her.

There is a huge difference between allowing her desires to overwhelm her initial hesitance and being tricked by the serpent into consuming the fruit.

There is no disagreement she wanted to be more like God. If you raise your children well, there is no greater compliment they can give you than to say, "When I grow up, I want to be just like you." Such a desire on their part is not rebellion; it is just the opposite. Adam and his wife were no different. They too wished to be more like their loving heavenly Father.

He Was Afraid Because . . .

When God asked Adam, "Where are you?," Adam replied:

> "I heard the sound of you in the garden, and I was afraid because I was naked, and I hid myself" (Genesis 3:10).

Some commentaries say Adam answered with an evasive half-truth. His nakedness, like his fear, resulted from his rebellion and the knowledge of his sinful state. The whole truth, according to these commentaries: Adam was afraid because of his disobedience.

There are several reasons for questioning this interpretation. The author of Genesis presented a common thread of nakedness from 2:25 through 3:11. He took care to inform the reader of the couple's *unashamed* nakedness before they ate the fruit. Then, as an immediate consequence of this action, their eyes were opened, they knew they were naked, and in turn were so ashamed they sewed fig leaves into aprons to hide their nakedness. Finally, Adam's response to the Lord's first query as well as His follow-on question focused on nakedness. Why go to all this effort and leave it to the reader to somehow try to figure out the "real reason" for Adam's fear?

There is no question Adam's disobedience could create guilt and even shame. But how could it also generate feelings of nakedness? As shared earlier, many of us have had dreams where we found ourselves in public wearing only our birthday suit. Such a self-consciousness is not prompted by disobedience.

Adam and his wife had been naked before this incident. What opened their eyes was their *newly acquired* knowledge of good and evil. Any emotions of guilt or shame they had broken God's command would be more associated with their relationship with the Lord than their commitment to each other. So, the fact they initially clothed themselves to cover their nakedness indicates disobedience was likely not the hidden issue in Adam's reply.

> *Adam and his wife had been naked before this incident. What opened their eyes was their newly acquired knowledge of good and evil.*

It also seems odd the Lord didn't see through Adam's so-called evasive half-truth, and direct His question at the root of Adam's fears (1 Samuel 16:7). If Adam was hiding the real reason he was afraid—he disobeyed God's command—then a more appropriate query might have been: "What is this that you have done?" That question would have focused on his disobedient *act*. Instead, the Lord asked him, "Who told you that you were naked?" to help him realize *his own* perspective of their relationship had precipitated his fearful reaction—an ability gained by his newly acquired knowledge of good and evil.

Why the Tree?

Question: If God did not want Adam to eat the fruit of the tree of the knowledge of good and evil, and if eating it would result in such dire consequences, why did He plant it in the garden, and next to the tree of life?

Answer: Adam had to live by faith to please the Lord, just like all believers (Hebrews 11:5, 6).[3] Paul says three things abide forever: faith, hope and love (1 Corinthians 13:12, 13).

So, even after Jesus Christ returns and all believers possess glorified bodies, we will still live by faith.

There had to be a fork in the road in Eden's idyllic landscape, one that would test Adam's belief God's way was best for him. When his wife brought him fruit from the tree asking him to eat, he could have said: "Your point is well taken. My memory of the Lord's warning may not be accurate. However, let's wait until this afternoon when He comes to visit us and ask Him whether the serpent's version is correct."

Adam decided to believe his wife's account of the serpent's statements rather than trust his own recollection of God's admonition. Nevertheless, his actions do not imply rebellion against the Lord's command. Remember at that moment, Adam and his wife were the two most innocent people the world has ever known. Rebellion suggests they were already resisting the Lord's authority in some manner and chose this event to manifest their insurrection. There is no indication in the second or third chapters of Genesis their relationship with the Lord had soured to the point where it precipitated this open act of defiance.

> *Adam decided to believe his wife's account of the serpent's statements rather than trust his own recollection of God's admonition. Nevertheless, his actions do not imply rebellion against the Lord's command.*

What is clear: Adam made a decision based on this test of his faith. Our faith is always tested (Genesis 22:1–19; James 1:2–4; 1 Peter 1:6, 7). His choice made us all slaves to sin. But it also revealed the enormous magnitude of God's grace in redeeming us through faith.

Why Reexamination Is Important

If all we inherited from Adam was the ability to comprehend the disparity between good and evil, then a logical definition of sin would be the selection of evil over good, reducing it to a lifelong list of misdeeds. Sin did not enter the biblical literature in Genesis chapter 3, where it could have been associated with Adam's transgression. Chapter 4 linked sin to Cain's feelings of anger toward his brother and portrayed it as an adversary "crouching at the door."

Paul said this opponent—his *flesh*—resided in his members, subjugating him to the law of sin and death. It is therefore critical we acknowledge sin as both an antagonist "crouching at the door"—the knowledge of good and evil we inherited from Adam—as well as the wrongful acts emanating from this wellspring. It will take this more thorough recognition if we are to find total deliverance. And that freedom will come only through faith in the gospel of Jesus Christ.

Study Questions for Discussion

- Why is it unlikely the Lord added the phrase "neither shall you touch it" in a later communication with Adam and his wife?
  - Adam or his mate must have added this codicil. If she was the source:
    - she might have been voicing their growing resentment with God's constraint not to eat the fruit of this one tree. In light of the bounty the garden offered them and the relationship they had with God, was this a likely motivation? or,
    - she added the phrase to remind her to avoid contact with the tree. Is that reason as likely as a motivation by Adam to add the words to keep her from accidentally ingesting the fruit?
  - Is there another option for their behavior than a growing resentment for God's constraint not to eat the fruit of this one tree?
- Before she ate the fruit and gained the knowledge of

good and evil, could Adam's wife have exhibited "the desires of the flesh" (1 John 2:15, 16)?

- Could there be another motivation for wanting to "be like God" (Genesis 3:5)?
  - Explain her motivation in light of the fact the serpent deceived her.
  - Could this motivation have been part of the reason Adam was willing to eat the fruit?
  - Is there a difference between disobedience and rebellion even though Adam's disobedient transgression brought death to all his descendants?
- Why did God plant the tree of the knowledge of good and evil in the garden?
- Why is it important to understand sin as more than a list of our misdeeds?

Five
The Relationship of Faith

> Then the disciples came to Jesus privately and
> said, "Why could we not cast it out?" He said
> to them, "Because of your little faith. For truly
> I say to you, if you have faith like a grain of
> mustard seed, you will say to this mountain,
> 'Move from here to there,' and it will move,
> and nothing will be impossible for you" (Mat-
> thew 17:19, 20).

Have you ever been puzzled by this passage? When His

disciples asked Jesus why they couldn't heal the boy, He began

by saying their faith was too small. But in the next breath, Jesus

assured them if they had faith no bigger than a mustard seed,

nothing would be too difficult for them, even successfully or-

dering a mountain to move. It appears the disciples' faith was

not only small, it must have been smaller than a mustard seed!

If this interpretation is correct, then faith can be viewed

as a quantitative spiritual asset—the more faith we have, the

more likely we will experience God working in our lives. It is

a common assumption. Perhaps you too have concluded you

did not have enough faith because the Lord did not answer

your prayers. The apostles probably had a similar understand-

ing.

> The apostles said to the Lord, "Increase our
> faith!" And the Lord said, "If you had faith

like a grain of mustard seed, you could say to
this mulberry tree, 'Be uprooted and planted in the sea' and it would obey you" (Luke
17:5–7).

They witnessed a steady parade of miraculous wonders

as they accompanied Jesus, and compared with His faith, theirs

seemed inadequate. But this time, Christ did not indicate their

faith needed to be increased. He said even the smallest amount

of faith would uproot a mulberry tree and plant it in the sea.

What Is 'Little-Faith'?

Fortunately, there is a definition of *little faith* that can

solve the puzzle broached at the beginning of this chapter.

During the Sermon on the Mount, Jesus coined a single word

to describe the kind of faith associated with those in atten-

dance. This term is only found in Matthew and Luke and not

in any extra-biblical literature. It is a compilation of "little" and

"faith."[1] Since there are no other references for this word Jesus

invented outside these New Testament texts, it is important

to analyze the context in which it is first used to better under-

stand its meaning.

His sermon begins with the Beatitudes that adorn our

Sunday school walls with familiar phrases. Seeing them, we

can readily forget they were the initial portion of Christ's first major address to an immense gathering from all over Israel, drawn largely by His healing ministry.

Every person had a story and a reason for being there. They hoped Jesus would establish a medical clinic on the spot. Instead, He chose to focus on the kingdom of God and their place in it.

We won't expound on the sermon as a whole. As an alternative, we will view the segment in which Christ created the term "little-faith" through the eyes of a man in the crowd we will call Jared.

> *They hoped Jesus would establish a medical clinic on the spot. Instead, He chose to focus on the kingdom of God and their place in it.*

★ ★ ★ ★ ★

Jared lived in Capernaum and came from a long line of carpenters, or more accurately, house builders who built most homes with stone foundations and walls of clay brick, or stone. Only the rafters were of wood since timber was scarce in Israel, especially in Galilee. The walls were plastered inside and out and a stairwell or a ladder on the exterior provided access to the flat roof. During hot summer months, families commonly slept on the roof in the cooler open air.

Jared and his two younger brothers, Caleb and Hiram, apprenticed with their father. There was so much to learn: how to square, peck, draft, cut, and lay stone; build clay brick walls and plaster them to repel the rain; cut and position the rafters, and then cover them with smaller brushwood and layers of clay. Finally, they compacted the roof assembly with a heavy stone roller—a task repeated after every rainy season.[2]

As the eldest, Jared's household included his widowed mother Dinah, his wife Rachel, two sons Obed and Jonathan, and his daughter Miriam. He was also the most knowledgeable about their craft and acted as the foreman at their job site.

That was until a few weeks ago, when Jared hurt his back lifting a rafter into place. At first, he shrugged it off and continued working. Nevertheless, by evening, the intense pain ruled out climbing the stairs to sleep on the roof.

Doctors weren't much help. They prescribed bed rest and thought he might be able to return to work in a few months. Unfortunately, the beginning of summer signaled the prime building season before the winter rains began in earnest. The three brothers formed an incredibly competitive team for new jobs. Now his back severely restricted Jared's capacity to help.

Nights were the worst. Sequestered in his home's interior, he was hot and sweaty, and no amount of turning on his bed would yield a comfortable position for long.

Then there were the flies—annoying pests that kept landing on his face no matter how many times he tried to shoo them away. They irritated him, especially when they crawled in his ears and mouth. And sleep eluded him largely because he couldn't keep his mind from rehearsing what might happen if his back did not heal completely.

Regrettably, his father also injured his back, and the family suffered greatly for it. Jared was still young and inexperienced when it happened. Pain curtailed most apprentice education to tasks around their house. So, years passed before Jared and his brothers reestablished their father's business.

Admittedly, he was a little jealous of his healthy brothers even though they were doing everything imaginable to assist his family. And as raw apprentices, Obed and Jonathan offered little more than basic labor to help fill the void.

Their rabbi came to the house several times to encourage everyone. *If God would respond to their prayers and restore his back,* Jared reasoned, *he might be able to return to work in time to save the season.* Jared's customers believed in his skills and knew he could construct any new home before the winter rains returned.

Jared tried to go to their job site to supervise, but the journey exacerbated his back pain. So, as an alternative, the brothers convened every evening after dinner to discuss the next day's assignments.

One morning before sunrise, Caleb burst into Jared's home. "Joshua[3] is here in Capernaum again and will be at Mount Eremos[4] later today," he said, completely out of breath. "He just got back from a tour throughout Galilee and enormous crowds are following him because he has been curing every disease and affliction."

"You know I can't travel that far!" retorted Jared. "Riding in our cart early last week aggravated my back so much I was miserable for days."

"Look, brother," Caleb answered, responding to Jared's dismissive tone. "Joshua is a fellow carpenter. He knows the dangers of our profession and may take extra notice of your condition. At least it's worth a shot."

"What's all the commotion?" Rachel asked as she hurried into the room and joined Caleb, urging her husband to go. "Perhaps Joshua is an answer to our prayers."

"OK, I'll try, if you promise to go slowly," Jared said, though obviously with reluctance.

The cart bumped and creaked along the dusty dirt road and then through a meadow as they approached a gigantic gathering. "Has Joshua started healing people yet?" asked Jonathan as they jostled their way toward the front of the crowd. Someone shook his head and pointed to a figure walking away from them up the side of Mount Eremos with a few other men following him.

"That must be Joshua with his disciples," offered another person.

Joshua turned and faced the multitude, then sat down and began to speak:

"Blessed are the poor in spirit, for theirs is the kingdom of heaven."

Jared strained to hear above the noise of the people and cart animals around him. *I'll be more than poor in spirit if my back doesn't improve*, he thought as his mind wondered back to those miserable years of hardship when his father couldn't work. By the time he refocused, Joshua was saying:

"Blessed are the meek, for they shall inherit the earth."

Jared didn't want to be too critical, but again thought: *I don't want to inherit the earth. My worry is that I might need to sell my meager inheritance to pay bills if I can't go back to work.*

The combination of a colicky baby nearby and his back pain exacerbated by the cart ride made it difficult to concentrate. Joshua did impress Jared by not quoting famous rabbis to bolster his views. Yet the speech seemed too religious and impractical— at least there was little Jared identified with. And his boys were getting antsy waiting for Joshua to start healing people.

But then the sermon took on a more personal tone.

> "Therefore, I tell you, do not be anxious about your life, what you will eat or what you will drink, nor about your body, what you will put on. Is not life more than food and the body more than clothing? Look at the birds of the air . . . consider the lilies of the field . . . if God so clothes the grass of the field . . . will he not much more clothe you, O you of little faith? . . . Seek first the kingdom of God and his righteousness, and all these things will be added to you."

Jared was anxious about his life and even more worried about what tomorrow might bring if his back didn't heal. Joshua seemed to be saying the Lord would meet his needs even if he was not able to work. *Easy for an itinerant rabbi to say.* The throng accompanying him would make sure he had food, clothing, and shelter.

But no one cared for Jared other than his family members. And he was not the only carpenter in the region. With just a few new houses being built every year, the competition was fierce. If he didn't actively participate in the family business, others would surely be chosen to build or remodel the homes.

When Joshua stopped speaking, he and his disciples started back toward Capernaum. The large gathering trailed after him, hoping to witness more miracles, and Jared and his family were among them.

Jared tolerated a hasty ride back, enduring the jarring and pain just to keep up with everyone else. Joshua did stop to restore the health of a leper, but then continued on his way, and Jared soon realized his back would not be healed that day.

✶ ✶ ✶ ✶ ✶

Jared went home disappointed and feeling inadequate, but still clinging to the belief he and others had in his ability to care for himself and his loved ones if only his back could be restored to health.

What did Jesus mean when he chided: "O you of little faith?" Was He saying self-reliance was not compatible with the kingdom of Heaven? Let's examine the context again.

> "Therefore I tell you, do not be anxious about your life . . . Look at the birds of the air: they

neither sow nor reap nor gather into barns,
and yet your heavenly Father feeds them. . .
Consider the lilies of the field. . . . If God so
clothes the grass . . . will he not much more
clothe you, O you of little faith" (Matthew
6:25-30).

While it is true the birds do not sow, reap, or gather into

barns, neither do they simply sit on their perches and expect a

handout every day from the Lord. They participate in feeding

activities and God provides the rest. So it is not faith in one's

own abilities that is at issue.

Jared was not alone in wanting a miracle. Matthew

4:23–25 indicates the reason vast multitudes followed Jesus

to Mount Eremos: During His tour through Galilee, they

brought Him all the sick, those afflicted with various diseas-

es and pains, those oppressed by demons, and epileptics and

paralytics—and He cured them. So it was natural to assume

Christ would continue to heal large numbers.

The word *anxious* in His address is key. Anxiety, frus-

tration, and worry are signals we are not able to cope with the

circumstances we are facing.

In our anxiety, we may want the Lord to resolve the situ-

ation with *our* desired remedy without first learning what *His*

solution for us might be. It is ingrained in us to believe this way because our anxious feelings reveal an underlying sense of nakedness or inadequacy compared to what others are capable of accomplishing.

> *The word* anxious *in His address is key. Anxiety, frustration, and worry are signals we are not able to cope with the circumstances we are facing.*

Those in attendance at the Sermon on the Mount were not "seeking first the kingdom of God and His righteousness"—the Lord's plan for their lives. They assumed since Jesus healed others, He would relieve their anxiety by performing similar miracles for them as well. It is this kind of presumptive faith that Christ labeled "little-faith."

If this is the definition of little-faith, why did Jesus use it when His disciples asked Him to explain their inability to heal the boy? After all, the Lord authorized them to cure the sick, raise the dead, cleanse lepers, and cast out demons in Matthew 10:7, 8. Another account of this incident in Mark 9:14–29 provides the reason.

> And when they came to the disciples, they saw a great crowd around them, and scribes arguing with them. . . . And he asked them, "What are you arguing about with them?" And someone from the crowd answered him, "Teacher, I brought my son to you, for he has a spirit that makes him mute. And whenever it seizes him, it throws him down, and he foams and grinds his teeth and becomes rigid. So, I

asked your disciples to cast it out, and they
were not able." . . . And when he had entered
the house, his disciples asked him privately,
"Why could we not cast it out?" And he said
to them, "This kind cannot be driven out by
anything but prayer."

"Why couldn't *we*?" Did they assume Christ commissioned them with an unrestricted mandate to heal anyone?
When they couldn't cast the demon out of the boy, they felt
frustrated and naked in the eyes of the child's father and the
rest of the crowd. To cover their embarrassment, they quar-
reled with the scribes.

They witnessed Christ healing multitudes of people and
likely assumed He acted on His own authority by commission
from His Father. But Jesus said,

"Truly, truly, I say to you, the Son can do
nothing of his own accord, but only what he
sees the Father doing" (John 5:19).

The disciples needed to adopt this posture as well. Earlier, they were granted authority to heal. Now, they presumed
they could perform the same remedy by urging God to deliver
the boy without first asking Him through prayer if that was
His will. This too was little-faith.

The futility of little-faith is apparent when Satan tempted
Jesus to exercise His own authority. After leading Him to a
pinnacle of the temple, Satan asked Christ to prove He was

the Son of God. "Throw yourself down, claim Psalm 90:11, 12, and the Lord will command His angels to save you." But Jesus replied, "You shall not put your God to the test"—meaning God would not be coerced into obeying someone else even if that person was His Son.

What Is Real Faith?

If little-faith is impotent, real faith, no matter how small, can accomplish anything. How is this possible? To answer that question, let's briefly consider Abraham, the paragon of faith.

> The word of the Lord came to Abram in a vision: "Fear not, Abram, I am your shield; your reward shall be very great." But Abram said, "O Lord God, what will you give me, for I continue childless, and the heir of my house is Eliezer of Damascus?" . . . And behold, the word of the Lord came to him: "This man shall not be your heir, your very own son shall be your heir." And he brought him outside and said, "Look toward heaven, and number the stars . . . So shall your offspring be." And he believed the Lord, and he counted it to him as righteousness (Genesis 15:1–6).

Verse six has a special place in Paul's writings[5] for good reason. Three words—*believed, counted,* and a noun form of *righteous*—enter the biblical literature[6] here. This Scripture is so familiar, we can overlook why it is located here and not associated with God's previous revelations.

> *Three words*—believed, counted, *and a noun form of* righteous—*enter the biblical literature here.*

For example, in Genesis chapter 6, the wickedness of humanity escalated to the point where the Lord decided to repopulate the earth with Noah and his family. God appeared to Noah and gave him instructions to build the ark. When it was completed:

> . . . the Lord said to Noah, "Go into the ark, you and all your household, for I have seen that you are righteous' before me in this generation" (Genesis 7:1).

Doubtless, Noah believed God or he would not have gone into the ark with his family. But the author of Genesis did not state that Noah's belief was counted to him as righteousness. That came many generations later, with Abram. The Lord said to the patriarch:

> "Go from your country and your kindred and your father's house to the land that I will show you. And I will make you a great nation." . . . So, Abram went as the Lord had told him (Genesis 12:1–4).

Again, Abram believed God or he would not have traveled to Canaan. However, the writer of Genesis still did not say in that encounter, Abram's faith was counted as righteousness.

The Lord had asked Noah to build an ark and Abram to leave his homeland and journey to Canaan. So, their belief in God's faithfulness was followed by action to carry out His directives.

The author of Genesis waited to inscribe the words of 15:6 because, in this verse, the Lord did not ask Abram to *do anything*. It is an elegant definition of the relationship of faith separate from any follow-on activity:

1. The Lord revealed His plan to Abram;

2. Abram believed God would accomplish what He revealed; and,

3. The Lord counted Abram's trust in Him as righteousness.

There is no chance someone reading this account would mistakenly assume righteousness was counted to Abram based on anything he accomplished, but only on his belief in God's faithfulness.[8]

Most of the time, God instructs a person to perform some work, and their actions demonstrate their belief in His revelation. So, James's admonition—"faith without works is dead" (James 2:17)—does not contradict this verse or any of Paul's writings.

A subsequent question can be asked of this text: how was righteousness counted to Abram? Did his character suddenly change so he no longer committed any transgressions against God or his neighbors? Obviously not! In 2 Corinthians 5:21, Paul writes:

> For our sake he made him to be sin who knew no sin, so that in him we might become the righteousness of God.

This Scripture does not apply only to Christians. When the Jews challenged Christ's credentials, He replied:

> "Your father Abraham rejoiced that he would see my day. He saw it and was glad." So, the Jews said to him, "You are not yet fifty years old, and have you seen Abraham?" Jesus said to them, "Truly, truly, I say to you, before Abraham was, I am" (John 8:56–58).

Jesus participated in the relationship of faith with their father. Why did Abram rejoice to see His day? Because *seeing* that day meant Christ's death and resurrection applied to him. It was the righteousness of God, made possible through the events of the day their father saw, that was counted to Abram. The Lord clothes all believers in His righteousness through the relationship of faith.[9]

Two Examples of Real Faith

A Leper

When Jesus concluded the Sermon on the Mount and was on His way to Capernaum, a leper approached him. This man had been watching from the edge of the crowd and knew Christ healed all manner of illnesses. Rather than assume Jesus would also heal him, the leper asked "Lord, if you will, you can make me clean." By first asking if it was God's will that he be clean and expressing belief in Christ's ability to cleanse him, the leper displayed real faith and was rewarded by being cured of his disease.

A Centurion

When Jesus entered Capernaum, several elders of the Jews begged Him to heal a centurion's servant, beloved by his owner; the servant was sick and near death. This man loved Israel and even built the town's synagogue! While Christ was still on His way, the centurion sent friends saying,

> "Lord, do not trouble yourself, for I am not worthy to have you come under my roof. Therefore I did not presume to come to you. But say the word, and let my servant be healed. For I too am a man set under authority, with solders under me, and I say to one, 'Go', and he goes, and to another, 'Come', and he comes" (Luke 7:6–8).

Jesus marveled at this response and said to the crowd following Him, "I tell you, not even in Israel have I found such faith." Even though the centurion was held in high esteem by the Jews, as a Gentile he respected their culture. He did not presume to come on his own or expect Christ to enter his house. Nor did he assume Jesus would heal his servant simply because He had healed others.

Based on his experience as a centurion, he *did* believe that if Christ said the word—if healing was part of God's plan for his servant—it would be carried out without the need for Jesus to set foot in his house. This Gentile became a model of the relationship of faith for the rest of us.

Faith and Healing

Jared came to Mount Eremos that day along with many others who hoped Jesus would heal them. They went home disappointed because of their little-faith.

Healing and other miracles have always been part of God's way of bearing witness to the Gospel.[10] One passage that addresses healing is James 5:14, 15.

> Is anyone among you sick? Let him call for the elders of the church, and let them pray over him, anointing him with oil in the name of the Lord. And the prayer of faith will save the one who is sick and the Lord will raise him up.

On the surface, we might think if a sick person calls for the elders/leaders of the church and they pray over him, anointing him with oil in the name of the Lord, that God would stretch out His hand to heal.

But let's look at this text more closely. James indicates the elders' *prayer of faith* will cure the sick. A prayer of faith implies the elders received prior indication of the Lord's desire to restore the health of the individual. So, once again, we cannot presume the elders can coerce God to do their bidding no matter how hard they pray or how worthy the situation seems to be for such an expression of the Lord's mercy and grace. That posture is little-faith.

> *We cannot presume the elders can coerce God to do their bidding no matter how hard they pray or how worthy the situation seems to be for such an expression of the Lord's mercy and grace. That posture is little-faith.*

* * * * *

A Personal Testimony

Ralph was an elder in our church. He awoke one morning to excruciating pain in his lower abdomen. Images, taken at the hospital, confirmed his doctor's suspicion that he was suffering from a kidney stone too large to pass. So the physician prescribed an analgesic to ease the constant agony. After several weeks trying to dissolve the stone through medication with no success, his doctor scheduled Ralph for surgery.

He checked in to the hospital the night before so additional images could be taken to better locate the kidney stone and determine its exact size. Ralph was in such debilitating pain, he called me, asking for our elders to come and pray in accordance with James's guidelines.

My wife, Miriam, and I and several elders gathered around his bed and asked the Lord for His will in this situation. Miriam felt God was telling her He wanted to crush the stone so it could pass. Not being an elder, she asked Him silently to confirm His leading by sharing it with the elders.

She hardly finished praying when Al and Scotty spoke up saying they felt the Lord wanted to crush the stone so it could pass. Miriam bore witness to their conviction and we all prayed for Ralph, anointing him with oil.

Soon afterward, a nurse entered the room, put Ralph in a wheelchair and wheeled him away for imaging. We all waited in the room—expecting.

After about half an hour, the nurse returned

with Ralph beaming from ear to ear. He was going home! The radiologist found no stones in his kidneys—only fine grains like sand that would easily pass.

* * * * *

This chapter has focused on the faith relationships of individuals. The next chapter will delve into God's gracious promises available to everyone through faith—promises that are at the heart of the Gospel.

Study Questions for Discussion

- What is little-faith (Matthew 6:30)?

  - Have you ever thought your faith was too small because God did not answer your prayers?

  - Have you ever been tempted to *claim* a Bible verse so God would answer your prayer?

  - What does worry and anxiety tell us about our solutions to the issues we are facing?

  - Why do we often pray for God to remedy the situation using our solutions?

  - What is the difference between bringing our requests to God and bringing our solutions (Philippians 4:6)?

- What is real faith?

  - How can real faith, no matter how small, move *mountains*?

  - Why did God wait until His encounter with Abram in Genesis 15:6 to share the way real faith works?

  - The Lord *counted* Abram's trust in Him as righteousness. In your own words, what does the word "counted" mean?

- How does God count righteousness to all believers?

- Can you recall a time when you witnessed God's gracious healing power?

  - What were the circumstances?

Six
Free Indeed!

Amazing grace (how sweet the sound)
that saved a wretch like me!
I once was lost, but now am found,
was blind, but now I see.
– John Newton (1779)[1]

"Amazing Grace," sung to an old Appalachian folk tune, is one of the most popular Gospel hymns in the United States. It is in virtually every hymnal and religious songbook.

You likely know the lyrics by heart, and the melody may even bring back fond memories. But do the words of the hymn evoke the same response? Was there ever a time when you honestly felt like a wretched person, lost and blind? John Newton penned those lyrics while remembering his profligate lifestyle as a sailor and captain of a slave ship. Few of us experience such a dissolute existence.

Perhaps the thrust of this hymn would apply to derelicts, winos, and drug addicts on skid row—but hardly to anyone in your church, let alone *you*. To fit this mold, a person must either be really bad or his life must be in shambles.

"Sinners" or "Good People?"

The Christian Gospel has little relevance in our society because the vast majority do not see themselves as "sinners." As long as sin is viewed as a list of misdeeds, and repentance as the need to confess and feel remorse for those sins, many will reply that they, and most folks they know, are "good people." They simply do not see any need for salvation.

If we don't wrestle with the full ramifications of sin, then we diminish our perception of salvation as well. We may believe all we inherited from Adam was the ability to choose between good and evil and that God's redemption in Jesus Christ paid the penalty for our bad choices. If such were the case, it would be like a judge who chooses to improve the way people drive by paying for speeding and parking tickets. But more is required: in order to modify a person's driving habits or overall lifestyle, it is necessary to reform behavior.

Paul was not living a life of drunken debauchery and licentiousness when he wrote, "Wretched man that I am, who can deliver me from this body of death?" (Romans 7:24). He was God's chosen apostle to the Gentiles crying out in anguish at his ongoing inability to master the law of sin and death waging war against him and making him its unwilling servant.

However, having penned his frustration, he went on to answer his own question.

> "Thanks be to God through Jesus Christ our Lord! So, then, <u>I myself serve the law of God with my mind, but with my flesh I serve the law of sin</u>" (Romans 7:25, *emphasis mine*).

On the surface, it appears Paul was no better off. On the one hand, with his mind, he continued to do what he believed was right according to the law of God. On the other hand, his adversary, armed with the knowledge of good and evil Paul had inherited from Adam, continued to force him to serve the law of sin. But Paul went on to explain how the Lord solved this dichotomy.

> There is therefore now <u>no condemnation for those who are in Christ Jesus</u>. For the law of the Spirit of life <u>has set you free in Christ Jesus</u> from the law of sin and death. For God has done what the law, weakened by the flesh, could not do. By sending his own Son <u>in the likeness of sinful flesh</u> and for sin he condemned sin in the flesh, in order that <u>the righteousness requirement of the law</u> might be fulfilled in us, who walk not according to the flesh but according to the Spirit (Romans 8:1–4, *emphasis mine*).

If Paul continued to serve the law of sin with his flesh, how did he not stand condemned under the very law he served with his mind? Notice the law of the Spirit of *life* is contrasted with the law of sin and *death*. The serpent had said, "You will become *like God*, knowing good and evil." Even though the Lord created Adam and Eve in His image, He made them without the ability to comprehend this knowledge.

The serpent was correct to indicate the Lord had this aptitude. But he deceived the first couple into believing they would become more *like God* by gaining this understanding. By eating the fruit, they hoped to grow closer to their Father. Instead, because of this new acquisition, they compared their individual differences with their mate and with the Lord. The feelings of nakedness these comparisons produced resulted in relational and spiritual death—separating them from the Lord and from each other and fulfilling God's warning: "In the day you eat of it you shall surely die."

> *The serpent was correct to indicate the Lord had this aptitude. But he deceived the first couple into believing they would become more like God by gaining this understanding.*

Jesus: The Only Sinless Son of Adam

Like Paul, Jesus was born a son of Adam. So through His birth, He inherited the knowledge of good and evil. Paul can say Jesus was born *in the likeness of sinful flesh* because He was also God incarnate. Since He always possessed this capability, it did not create in Him feelings of nakedness.

By living His life as the son of Adam *and* God, He condemned sin in the flesh (in His Adam nature). The potentially devastating inheritance He received from Adam did not cause Jesus to experience relational or spiritual death. By doing so, He became the only son of Adam to live a life *free* from the law of sin and *death*. He was also the only son of Adam whose lifestyle mirrored the law of the Spirit of *life*.

Jesus Took Our Place in Judgment

Unlike Jesus, we are all slaves of sin. So, how can we be liberated from the law of sin and death? The answer is in Paul's phrase "the righteous requirement of the law." The Lord is a righteous God and as such *must* judge sin. He cannot simply forgive our offenses as an act of grace and mercy without violating His righteous nature.

If that option were viable, His Son would not have had to die on the cross. The night before He died, Jesus spent much of the night in earnest prayer with His Father, trying to find another way—but there was no other way.

> And he withdrew from them about a stone's throw, and knelt down and prayed, saying, "Father, if you are willing, remove this cup from me. Nevertheless, not my will, by yours be done." And there appeared to him an angel

from heaven, strengthening him. And being in agony he prayed more earnestly, and his sweat became like great drops of blood falling down to the ground (Luke 22:41-44).

Some see in Genesis 3:21—where the Lord made garments for the couple from skins—as the first instance of a pattern of atonement involving the substitutable sacrifice of an animal's life.

In Exodus 25:17–22, God gave Moses instructions to build the ark of the covenant with the mercy seat resting on top of the ark. On the day of atonement, the high priest brought the sacrificial blood into the innermost region of the tabernacle—and later the temple—and sprinkled the blood on the mercy seat as an offering for himself and the unintentional sins of all the people (Hebrews 9:7). The shedding of blood was necessary because as a righteous judge, God had to condemn sin (Hebrews 9:22).

> *Some see in Genesis 3:21—where the Lord made garments for the couple from skins—as the first instance of a pattern of atonement involving the substitutable sacrifice of an animal's life.*

Sprinkling blood on the mercy seat was described as a sacrificial act of propitiation[2] (a worthy synonym for this word is *appeasement*). The animal had to be a perfect specimen, and

God substituted its blameless life as an oblation for the lives of the Israelites. This annual ritual foreshadowed Christ's sacrifice on our behalf.

> For all have sinned and fall short of the glory of God, and are justified by his grace as a gift, through the redemption that is in Christ Jesus, whom God put forward as a <u>propitiation by his blood</u>, to be received by faith. This was to <u>show God's righteousness</u>, because in his divine forbearance he had passed over former sins. It was to <u>show his righteousness</u> at the present time, so that he might be just and the justifier of the one who has faith in Jesus (Romans 3:23-26, *emphasis mine*).

As the only son of Adam who did not sin and fall short of the glory of God, Jesus became God's gracious gift, put forward as a faultless propitiation by His sacrifice on the cross. God's righteousness was manifested through judging His Son instead of every person who ever lived either before or after Christ's death and resurrection.[3]

Christ's Sacrifice Fulfilled God's Righteousness

How did God's righteous judgment of His Son impart His righteousness to all believers? Paul answers this question in 2 Corinthians 5:21.

> For our sake he made him to be sin for us who knew no sin, so that in him we might become the righteousness of God.

To use the words of Genesis 15:6, during the sacrificial act of propitiation on the cross, the Lord "counted" our sin to Jesus so that, through His death, God "counts" His righteousness to all who believe.

The thought of being cursed and thereby separated from His Father was abhorrent to Jesus during His night of prayer in the Garden of Gethsemane.

> "Christ redeemed us from the curse of the law by becoming a curse for us—for it is written, 'Cursed is everyone who is hanged on a tree'—so that in Christ Jesus the blessings of Abraham might come to the Gentiles, so that we[4] might receive the promised Spirit through faith" (Galatians 3:13, 14, *emphasis mine*).

We hear the dreadful anguish in His voice when Jesus uttered these words from the cross.

> Now from the sixth hour there was darkness over all the land until the ninth hour. And about the ninth hour Jesus cried out with a loud voice, saying, "Eli Eli, lema sabachthani?" that is, "My God, my God, why have you forsaken me" (Matthew 27:45, 46)?

Of all the words Christ spoke from the cross, these reflect the darkness that had enveloped His tormented soul. His desperate cry was heart-wrenching. In the midst of this moment, He chose to quote Psalm 22:1 to convey to us His dreadful feelings of separation from His Father—that He was experiencing spiritual and relational death.

Jesus knew why His Father had forsaken Him. It was devastating to Him nonetheless. Earlier, He had revealed to His disciples that His soul was troubled by the prospect of becoming sin for us. He also assured them it was precisely for this hour He had come.

> Now among those who went up to worship at the feast were some Greeks. So these came to Philip, who was from Bethsaida in Galilee, and asked him, "Sir, we wish to see Jesus." Philip went and told Andrew, Andrew and Philip went and told Jesus. And Jesus answered them, "The hour has come for the Son of Man to be glorified. . . . <u>Now is my soul troubled. And what shall I say? 'Father, save me from this hour?' But for this purpose I have come to this hour. 'Father, glorify your name.'"</u> Then a voice came from heaven: "I have glorified it, and I will glorify it again" (John 12:20-28, emphasis mine).

> When Jesus had finished all these sayings, he said to his disciples, "You know that after two days the Passover is coming, and the Son of Man will be delivered up to be crucified" (Matthew 26:1, 2).

In the waning hours before sunset, Jesus knew His ordeal would soon be over.

> After this, Jesus, knowing that all was now finished, said (to fulfill the Scripture), "I thirst." A jar full of sour wine stood there, so they put a sponge full of the sour wine on a hyssop branch and held it to his mouth. When Jesus had received the sour wine, he said, "It is finished," and he bowed his head and gave up his spirit (John 19:28-30).

> Then Jesus calling out with a loud voice, said,

"Father, into your hands I commit my spirit!" And having said this he breathed his last. Now when the centurion saw what had taken place, he praised God, saying, "Certainly this man was innocent!" (Luke 23:46, 47)

Paul summarizes how Jesus Christ took our place in judgment in Romans 5:6-11 (*emphasis mine*).

For while we were still weak, at the right time Christ died for the ungodly. For one will scarcely die for a righteous person—though perhaps for a good person one would dare even to die—but God shows his love for us in that while we were still sinners, Christ died for us. Since, therefore, we have now been justified by his blood, much more shall we be saved by him from the wrath of God. For if while we were enemies we were reconciled to God by the death of his Son, much more, now that we are reconciled, shall we be saved by his life. More than that, we also rejoice in God through our Lord Jesus Christ, through whom we have now received reconciliation.

How Can One Die for All?

How can the sacrifice of one individual reconcile all the children of Adam who are under the sentence of death? After all, if such a thing were possible and an innocent person could take the place of another individual on death row, only one human being could be set free.

Paul answered this question by saying all believers participated in the crucifixion of Jesus Christ.

I have been crucified with Christ. It is no longer I who live, but Christ who lives in me. And the life I now live in the flesh I live by faith in the Son of God, who loved me and gave himself for me (Galatians 2:20).

Obviously, Paul did not pass away when Jesus died. So, how was he—and how are we—crucified with Christ? Further, what kind of life is Paul talking about? Since he did not die, he must not be referring to his physical life.

The author of Genesis wrote that God created us in His image and likeness.

Then God said, "Let us make <u>man in our image, after our likeness.</u>" . . . So, God created man <u>in his own image</u>, in the image of God he created him; male and female he created them (Genesis 1:26, 27, *emphasis mine*).

Jesus said:

"<u>God is spirit</u>, and those who worship him must worship in spirit and truth" (John 4:24, *emphasis mine*).

> *Obviously, Paul did not pass away when Jesus died. So, how was he—and how are we—crucified with Christ?*

Taken together, we know that God did not create our physical bodies in His image and likeness. He would form a body for Adam out of the dust of the ground (Genesis 2:7). Paul makes a clear distinction that although our bodies are necessary, as spiritual beings, they are separate from our life and will pass away when we die.

> For we know that <u>if the tent that is our earthly home is destroyed</u>, we have a building from God, a house not made with hands, eternal in the heavens. . . . We know that <u>while we are at home in the body</u>, we are away from the Lord (2 Corinthians 5:1-6, *emphasis mine*).

The author of Hebrews says concerning Jesus:

> He is the radiance of the glory of God and the <u>exact imprint</u> of his nature (Hebrews 1:3, *emphasis mine*).

Since Christ is God incarnate, His is the *exact imprint* of God's nature. The Lord created us without the knowledge of good and evil.[5] So, our nature is not His exact imprint. However, He did create us in His *image and likeness*. Because of this "familial" image, the Lord can adopt us as His sons and daughters through faith.

> "And I will be a father to you, and <u>you shall be sons and daughters to me</u>," says the Lord Almighty (2 Corinthians 6:18, *emphasis mine*).

> For <u>those whom he foreknew he also predestined to be conformed to the image of his Son</u>, in order that he might be the firstborn among many brothers (Romans 8:29, *emphasis mine*).

We all sin and fall short of the glory of God and, as such, experience relational and spiritual death. For our sake, God made Christ to be sin for us who knew no sin. While it is true that Christ died on the cross and shed His own blood as our propitiation, the depth of His sacrifice is much more than His *physical* death. If that were the case, then His death would benefit only one other human being.

Instead, when Jesus became spiritually and relationally separated from His Father on the cross, God "counted" our relational and spiritual death as those of His Son. He could do so because, through faith, He had already conformed us to the image of His Son. Viewed from God's perspective, Christ's death became our death so that, "in Him," we might also become the righteousness of God.

Transformed By the Renewal of Our Mind

How can Paul serve the law of God with His mind without being thwarted by the opponent within? After all, there may be no condemnation for serving sin with his flesh, but how was he able to serve the law of God when his adversary could hamper him at every turn? He addresses this issue in Romans 12:1, 2 (*emphasis mine*).

> I appeal to you therefore, brothers, by the mercies of God, to present your bodies as a living sacrifice, holy and acceptable to God, which is your spiritual worship. Do not be conformed to this world, but <u>be transformed by the renewal of your mind</u>, that by testing you may discern what is the will of God, what is good and acceptable and perfect.

Paul begins this passage by reminding his readers of the mercies of God they received by faith through the death and resurrection of Jesus Christ. In light of the Lord's merciful and gracious redemption, he appeals to us to place our *bodies,* without reservation, at the disposal of God as living sacrifices to do with as He wills. This holy act is our form of continuous, spiritual worship.

Before considering the next two verbs in this passage, we need to understand a little about the original Greek language of the New Testament. Greek verbs can have one of three voices: active, middle, and passive. In English, there are only two: active and passive. A verb in the active voice means the subject performs the action while a verb in the passive voice means the subject receives the action. There are many shades to the middle voice in Greek. Its basic significance is that the subject participates in the action.[6] If Paul had used the active voice, he would appeal to us to not conform ourselves to the world. The middle voice yields the translation: do not "be conformed" to this world, meaning we participate but are not the only one taking part in this conformational activity. Our adversary is also a contributor, and before we were believers, enslaved us to the law of sin. Now, through faith, we no longer *need* to conform to this world because our old self was crucified with Christ.

> We know that <u>our old self was crucified with him</u> in order that the <u>body of sin might be brought to nothing</u>, so that we would <u>no longer be enslaved to sin</u>. For one who has died has been set free from sin. Now <u>if we have died with Christ</u>, we believe that we will also live with him. We know that Christ being raised from the dead, will never die again; death no longer has dominion over him. For the death he died he died to sin, once for all, but the life he lives he lives to God. So, <u>you must also consider yourselves dead to sin and alive to God in Christ Jesus</u> (Romans 6:6-11, *emphasis mine*).

Why is the body of sin brought to nothing? Because through faith, our old self—our spirit dwelling within our physical body—has been crucified with Christ. Sin cannot control a deceased person. In Romans chapter 7, Paul struggled mightily to overcome sin dwelling in his members—but could not. Those very actions indicate he was focusing on sin in his members—meaning he was alive to sin, not dead to sin as Romans 6:11 indicates. As long as he, or we, wrestle with the sinful habits we no longer wish to perform, our adversary will win because we are conforming to a way of life sin can control. To die to sin means we should not attempt in any way to resist sin any more than we would if we were lying (dead) in a pine box.

Returning to the last of the two verbs in Romans 12:2: "but *be transformed* by the renewing of your mind." This last verb is in the passive voice meaning the renewal of our mind is done *to us*—we do not actively participate in this ongoing activity.

Our English word *metamorphosis* comes from this Greek word; a quintessential example is the caterpillar-to-butterfly transformation. The caterpillar hatches from an egg and lives its existence by eating the foliage of flowering plants. It knows nothing of the way of life it will become as a butterfly—the ability to fly and dine on nectar rather than leaves. As it grows, it sheds its skin several times.

Then, one day, it attaches itself to the underside of a leaf or twig and molts one final time, its new skin hardening into a chrysalis.[7] Other than the act of attaching with a small thread of silk, this last molt starts out the same as the others. However, this time when it emerges it is a butterfly and not a caterpillar—a transformation created by its genes rather than by any active participation of its own! Instead of returning to the edge of a leaf to continue eating as it had before, the butterfly unfolds its wings and flies away to feed on highly nutritious nectar. The creature's entire perspective of the world is forever changed.

So, how are we *transformed* by the renewing of our minds? Jesus told His disciples He and His Father would make their home in us.

> "I will not leave you as orphans; <u>I will come to you</u>. Yet a little while and the world will see me no more, but you will see me. Because I live, you also will live. In that day you will know that I am in my Father, and you in me, <u>and I in you</u>. . . . if anyone loves me, he will keep my word, and my Father will love him, and <u>we will come</u> to him and make our home with him" (John 14:18-23, *emphasis mine*).

He also said He would send another Helper who would be in us and would guide us into all truth.

> "And I will ask the Father, and he will give you another Helper, to be with you forever, even the Spirit of truth . . . You know him, for he dwells with you and <u>will be in you</u>. . . . the Helper, the Holy Spirit, whom the Father will send in my name, <u>he will teach you all things</u>" (John 14:16-26, *emphasis mine*).

> "I still have many things to say to you, but you cannot bear them now. When the Spirit of truth comes, <u>he will guide you into all the truth</u>, for he will not speak on his own authority, <u>but whatever he hears he will speak</u>, and <u>he will declare to you the things that are to come</u>" (John 16:12-14, *emphasis mine*).

To use Proverbs 3:5, 6 as a template, when we encounter our life experiences, we should *not rely on our own understanding* to discern the will of God for us. Such an active posture would keep us enslaved to the law of sin and death.

Instead, we can acknowledge the presence of the Lord dwelling in us, and through prayer, ask for guidance. Jesus said both He and His Father will communicate their perception of the situation we face to the Holy Spirit. And the Spirit *will direct our paths* by revealing to us what He hears. In this way, we will be transformed by the renewal of our mind as we are enlightened by the revelations of the Holy Spirit. Paul associated this spiritual discernment and our renewal with the mind of Christ.

> The natural person does not accept the things of the Spirit of God, for they are folly to him, and he is not able to understand them because they are spiritually discerned. The spiritual person judges all things, but is himself to be judged by no one. "For who has understood the mind of the Lord so as to instruct him?" But we have the mind of Christ (1 Corinthians 2:14-16, *emphasis mine*).

Furthermore, just as the entire life of the caterpillar is changed by metamorphosis, our transformation involves much more than the renewal of our mind.

Walking in the Light

> This is the message we have heard from him and proclaim to you, that God is light, and in him is no darkness at all. If we say we have fellowship with him while we walk in darkness, we lie and do not practice the truth. But if we walk in the light, as he is in the light, we have fellowship with one another, and the blood of

Jesus his Son cleanses us from all sin. If we say we have no sin, we deceive ourselves, and the truth is not in us. If we confess our sins, he is faithful and just to forgive us our sins and to cleanse us from all unrighteousness (1 John 1:5-9, *emphasis mine*).

What does John mean when he urges us to walk in the light and not in darkness? When you find yourself in the dark, on unfamiliar terrain, how do your tread? Do you stride confidently, as though you can see everything in front of you, or do you cautiously test each step to make sure you don't fall into a hole or stumble over a rock?

The spiritual analogy to this kind of tentative movement is the person who carefully weighs every action taken to make sure it is the right thing to do. This reliance on our knowledge of good and evil inherited from Adam enslaves us to the law of sin and death. So, even though we might say we are trying our best to have fellowship with God by doing the right thing, we are actually walking in darkness and our actions betray our ignorance of the truth.

By considering ourselves dead to sin and alive to God in Christ Jesus, we move forward with our lives following Him *through faith* without the need or desire to test the correctness of our decisions. In this way, we walk in the light as He is in the light and we have fellowship with one another. When we do fall short, instead of trying to overcome our faults, we can confess our sins to the Lord, knowing He is faithful and just to forgive our sins, and that the blood of Jesus, our propitiation, cleanses us from every kind of wrong.

The word *cleanses* is a present tense verb meaning the blood of Jesus Christ is continuously purifying us. In fact, if we walk in the light as He is in the light, our fellowship with God, our confession of sin, and our cleansing from all unrighteousness are all *continuous*.

You Must Be Born Again

The words "in Christ Jesus" or "in him" occur many times in the Scriptures quoted in this chapter. They proclaim God's salvation is "in Christ Jesus" and is available through faith. So, how do we appropriate this redemption? A Pharisee named Nicodemus came to Jesus one night and the Lord told him he must be born again.

> Now there was a man of the Pharisees named Nicodemus, a ruler of the Jews. This man came to Jesus by night and said to him, "Rabbi, we know that you are a teacher come from God, for no one can do these signs that you do unless God is with him." Jesus answered him, "Truly, truly, I say to you, <u>unless one is born again, he cannot see the kingdom of God.</u>" Nicodemus said to him, "How can a man be born when he is old? Can he enter a second time into his mother's womb and be

born?" Jesus answered, "Truly, truly, I say to you, unless one is born of water and the Spirit, he cannot enter the kingdom of God. That which is born flesh is flesh, and <u>that which is born of the Spirit is spirit</u>. Do not marvel that I said to you, You must be born again" (John 3:1-7, *emphasis mine*).

When Nicodemus objected to the possibility of a person entering his mother's womb a second time, Jesus said He was not referring to a physical birth but the rebirth of Nicodemus's spirit.

We learned we are dead in our trespasses and sins (Ephesians 2:1), meaning our sin separates us (our spirit) from God and the only way to regain this connection is through faith in Jesus Christ. No amount of good works or attempts to obey God's law can renew this relationship. The law only reminds us we are incapable to overcoming the opponent within us (Romans 3:20)—the knowledge of good and evil—the wellspring of our separation. Furthermore, any attempt to conquer this adversary on our own only results in frustration, as Paul discovered (Romans 7:24).

> *When Nicodemus objected to the possibility of a person entering his mother's womb a second time, Jesus said He was not referring to a physical birth but the rebirth of Nicodemus's spirit.*

You might be thinking you are born again and can remember when it happened. But perhaps these words are new to you. The rebirth of our spirit is the entry into an ongoing relationship with the Lord through faith in Jesus Christ.

According to the definition of faith outlined in the previous chapter, the Lord promised Abram a son, and told him his progeny would be as countless as the stars. Abram believed God could fulfill His pledge, and the Lord counted Abram's trust in Him as righteousness. What promise can we believe in that reestablishes our relationship with the Lord and also justifies us?

According to the apostle Peter, God desires that all the descendants of Adam have a change of heart[8] and seek a relationship with Him.

> The Lord is not slow to fulfill his promise as some count slowness, but is patient toward you, not wishing that any should perish, <u>but that all should reach</u>[9] <u>repentance</u> (2 Peter 3:9, *emphasis mine*).

Because He wants everyone to repent, God offers salvation to every person through faith in His Son.

> For God so loved the world, that he gave his only Son, that <u>whoever believes in him</u> should not perish but have eternal life (John 3:16, *emphasis mine*).

Paul outlines the steps for a person to take to begin this new relationship.

> If you <u>confess with your mouth that Jesus
> is Lord and believe in your heart that God
> raised him from the dead, you will be saved</u>.
> For with the heart one believes and is justi-
> fied, and with the mouth one confesses and is
> saved (Romans 10:9, 10, *emphasis mine*).

The Greek verb tenses for *confess* and *believe* refer to a definite point in time rather than a continuous action. So, confessing that Jesus is Lord and believing God raised Him from the dead takes place at a particular time in a person's life and signals the moment of spiritual rebirth.

The process of confessing and believing underscores the meaning of repentance—the person is thereby expressing a true change of heart. Individuals may feel guilty for past sins. However, if they also see themselves as "good people," they may feel little or no contrition. Sincere repentance leads to the recognition they are separated from God and no longer want to live according to the law of sin and death.

Jesus Is Our Living Lord

Paul discovered that even as the apostle to the Gentiles he was incapable of thwarting the debilitating influence of the knowledge of good and evil he had inherited from Adam. The one individual who could, and can, is the only Son of Adam who lived a life unimpeded by the destructive consequences of this intellectual capacity—Jesus Christ, whom God raised from the dead and who lives forever, free from the constraints of death. So, it is imperative when we invite Christ to come into our life and reestablish our spiritual relationship with Him that we ask Him to take over and become our Lord. Only then can Jesus live His life in us and renew our minds, transforming us into the person—the *butterfly*—His Father wants us to be.

> Therefore, as you received Christ Jesus the Lord, so walk in him, <u>rooted and built up in him and established in the faith,</u> just as you were taught, abounding in thanksgiving (Colossians 2:6, 7, *emphasis mine*).

> "Behold, I stand at the door and knock. If anyone hears my voice and opens the door, I will come in to him and eat with him, and he with me" (Revelations 3:20).

> If the son sets you free, you are free indeed (John 8:36)!

It is imperative when we invite Christ to come into our life and reestablish our spiritual relationship with Him that we ask Him to take over and become our Lord. Only then can Jesus live His life in us and renew our minds, transforming us into the person—the butterfly—*His Father wants us to be.*

Your prayer of faith in God's promise to be born again can be as simple as: "Christ, take over my life." Or you may want to say it in your own words. The important thing is that the confession of your mouth expresses a sincere change of your heart.

A Personal Testimony

As you read in the introduction, my father and mother traveled over the Alcan highway from Phoenix to Alaska to homestead in the Matanuska Valley shortly after World War II. Wasilla was the nearest village where, according to the locals, 108 souls resided counting dogs and chickens.

I was only two and a half when we moved and it was another four years before my brother John arrived, followed by Mike, Ron, and Valerie. They were born close enough to be playmates. The only other boy my age lived more than six miles away—too far for any ongoing camaraderie. Our only regular contact was at school.

Wasilla had been established with a train station to support the gold and coal mines in the nearby Talkeetna Mountain range. Walt and Vivian Teeland's country store was the hub of daily life. Just down a boardwalk from Teeland's, the roadhouse offered meals and a place to stay. Further up the street, a small post office provided a link to the outside world, and then a few more steps brought you to a log cabin, Grange Hall, which served as the focal point of many social functions.

The local bar and dance hall was situated across the street from Teeland's, and up from there, Rose and Oscar Johnson had built a sauna where people also held meetings. The Presbyterian church and schoolhouse were a couple of streets behind the bar and served the families in the surrounding region.

My classmates included Larry Teeland and Helen Carter, daughter of the postmaster. They were the core of the "city kids"—I was a "country boy." So, even at school, I felt like an outsider with few friends since I went home after class on the bus.

One summer, dad was working part-time at Teeland's to earn extra money and I went to town with him to get a pair of tennis shoes. Several classmates were in the store and invited me to vacation Bible school. Having nothing else to do before dad's shift was over, I went with them.

I don't remember much about the lesson except the teacher used a felt board to tell the story of Joseph and his coat of many colors. The one thing that stuck with me was the feeling of belonging—of being part of the class—and I didn't want to leave. Even though I was invited to return the next day, there were many chores to do at home with dad away at work.

But that memory of belonging never left me, and by the time I was able to drive, I asked my parents if we could go to church. Since they had been raised Catholics, we began attending the Catholic church in Palmer.

Unfortunately, the parish priest drove down to Palmer from Anchorage for Sunday services, and he rarely succeeded in making it during the dead of winter or spring breakup. So, as often as not, our efforts to get ready and travel to Palmer were frustrated by the news the church service had been canceled. It didn't take long before we stopped going altogether. However, when we did attend, I never felt the same sense of belonging, even though I became an altar boy.[10]

I attended college at Alaska Methodist University in Anchorage and often helped serve mass at nearby Providence Hospital. Still, the sense of belonging eluded me. Then, in the spring of my senior year, Bill Bright, founder of Campus Crusade for Christ, spoke at our college. His speech centered around Campus Crusade's four spiritual laws and the need to invite Jesus Christ to sit on the throne of our lives.[11]

After he finished, I went up and told him I agreed with his message but wanted to go to confession to clean up my "house" before asking Christ to come in and take over. Mr. Bright assured me such actions were unnecessary and asked if there was a nearby room where we could pray.

In the college's small piano practice room, Bill led me in prayer to ask Jesus Christ to come into my life and be my Lord and Savior. That night, the feelings of wholeness and belonging returned—and have never left me.

It is my sincere hope if you have not made a similar commitment to Jesus Christ, you will do so.

Study Questions for Discussion

- How do you identify with the lyrics of "Amazing Grace?"

- Why do so many individuals consider themselves "good people?"

  - How do "good people" define sin?

- How can we serve the law of God with our mind if we continue to serve the law of sin with our flesh (Romans 7:25)?

- Paul says Jesus was born in the likeness of sinful flesh (Romans 8:3). What did he mean by that statement?

  - How could Jesus condemn sin in the flesh?

- Why can't God just forgive us as an act of His grace and mercy?

- Describe what Paul means when he says Jesus is our propitiation (Romans 3:25)?

  - How did Christ's death fulfill the righteousness of God?

- How can the death of one man—Jesus—count for the sins of all mankind (Galatians 2:20)?

- How can we serve the law of God with our mind

without being thwarted by sin that "dwells within us" (Romans 7:20, 12:1, 2)?

- How does walking in the light cleanse us from all sin (1 John 1:5-9)?

- Why is it necessary to be born again in order to establish a relationship with God (John 3:1-7)?

  - Recalling the definition of real faith from the previous chapter, how can a person accept Jesus Christ as their Lord and Savior *by faith* (John 3:16; 2 Peter 3:9)?

    - Why is it imperative that we invite Jesus Christ to be the Lord of our lives as well as our Savior?

Seven
Walking in the Way

In the last chapter, we focused on the importance of establishing a relationship by faith with Christ as the Lord of our lives. Jesus called this spiritual beginning being born again—an event representing the first moments when we emerge from our own "chrysalis" to start a new life of fellowship with God.

The Lord told Noah to build an ark and promised Abram he would be the father of a multitude. God also has a definite plan for each one of us to be received by faith, just as He had for Noah and Abram. That objective is much more than our salvation. We all have a unique role to play in the kingdom of Heaven.

How do we receive His guidance so we can be sure of His blueprint for us and live by it? There are three avenues the Lord uses to assist us in our walk with Him: the Bible, God's voice, and His peace.

> *There are three avenues the Lord uses to assist us in our walk with Him: the Bible, God's voice, and His peace.*

The Bible

Here was one of my favorite Hebrew texts when I was a young Christian.

> "Just as I was with Moses, so I will be with you. I will not leave you or forsake you. Be strong and courageous, for you shall cause this people to inherit the land that I swore to their fathers to give them. Only <u>be strong and very courageous, being careful to do according to all the law that Moses my servant commanded you</u>. Do not turn from it to the right hand or to the left, that you may have good success wherever you go. This Book of the Law shall not depart from your mouth, but you shall meditate on it day and night, so that you may be careful to do according to all that is written in it. For then you will make your way prosperous, and then you will have good success. <u>Have I not commanded you? Be strong and courageous. Do not be frightened, and do not be dismayed, for the Lord your God is with you wherever you go</u>" (Joshua 1:5-9, *emphasis mine*).

Joshua was Moses' disciple throughout the Exodus and witnessed firsthand how the Lord mentored Moses. Now, the mantle of leadership had passed to Joshua, and he faced the intimidating challenge of bringing the children of Israel into the Promised Land to possess it in fulfillment of God's promise to Abraham. No amount of training could fully prepare him knowing Moses was no longer there for support.

Joshua's new responsibilities doubtlessly overwhelmed him because God encouraged him more than once to be strong and courageous. In addition, the Lord reminded him he must meditate on Moses' Book of the Law to succeed wherever he went. Even though the Lord would be with him as He was with Moses, Joshua knew he must use utmost care to observe everything written in the Law so he could prosper and be successful in the tasks ahead.

Unfortunately, if we read this text through the filter of the knowledge of good and evil we inherited from Adam, we reduce Moses' Book of the Law to a compilation of divine rules and regulations to be explicitly followed so we can live a victorious life. The Scriptures are foundational. Without them, we would be building our relationship with the Lord based on our own understanding.

However, they are much more than legal requirements to be religiously observed. Moses realized the Israelites would come to this mistaken conclusion and subsequently believe obeying so many statutes would be a daunting if not impossible task. So, when he finished inscribing the Law a second time, Moses addressed them with these words.

> "For this commandment that I command you today is not too hard for you, neither is it far off. It is not in heaven, that you should say, 'Who will ascend to heaven for us and bring it to us, that we may hear it and do it?' Neither is it beyond the sea, that you should say, 'Who

will go over the sea for us and bring it to us, that we may hear it and do it?' But the word is very near you. It is in your mouth and in your heart, so that you can do it" (Deuteronomy 30:11–14, *emphasis mine*).

If the last verse sounds familiar, it is because it is mirrored in the Romans passage quoted in the previous chapter.

If you confess with your mouth that Jesus is Lord and believe in your heart that God raised him from the dead, you will be saved. For with the heart one believes and is justified, and with the mouth one confesses and is saved (Romans 10:9, 10, *emphasis mine*).

Taken together, we can see the primary reason Moses recorded the Law was to encourage people to search for and find a relationship with God through faith. Any attempt to obey all the Law's legal requirements would yield the realization that full compliance was impossible (Romans 3:20). Once a person recognized righteousness could not be obtained through obedience to the Law's legal demands, the individual could aspire to be counted as righteous through faith in a way similar to Abraham.

The Scriptures are foundational. Without them, we would be building our relationship with the Lord based on our own understanding.

Jesus clarified the focus of the Law when asked by a Pharisee to identify the greatest commandment. He was expecting

Christ to respond with one of the codified statutes. Jesus went much further.

> But when the Pharisees heard that he had silenced the Sadducees, they gathered together. And one of them, a lawyer, asked him a question to test him. "Teacher, which is the great commandment in the Law?" And he said to him, "You shall love the Lord your God with all your heart and with all your soul and with all your mind. This is the great and first commandment. And a second is like it: You shall love your neighbor as yourself. <u>On these two commandments depend all the Law and the Prophets</u>" (Matthew 22:34–40, *emphasis mine*).

Here is Paul's assessment of the Bible.

> All scripture is breathed out by God[1] and is profitable for teaching, for reproof, for correction, and for training in righteousness, that the man of God may be complete, equipped for every good work (2 Timothy 3:16).

Another function of Scripture is found in the Psalms.

> Your word is a lamp to my feet and a light to my path (Psalm 119:105).

Today, we can go for a walk outside after dark with the help of a flashlight or street lamps. In the not-too-distant past, folks carried a lantern. If the lamp illuminated the darkness with a candle or an oil wick, it was often suspended by a chord so it could swing close to the ground. The light from this device helped the person view the path immediately in front of them. But it did not shine more than a few steps ahead.

In the same way, the Bible illuminates our spiritual path by revealing an instruction or a person with whom we can identify, bolstering our relationship with God. However, it does not disclose the Lord's specific, long-term intention for each one of us. He divulges that blueprint by communicating as He did with those in the Scriptures who believed in Him.

God's Voice

> Trust in the Lord with all your heart, and do not lean on your own understanding. In all your ways acknowledge him, and he will make straight your paths (Proverbs 3:5).

Recalling the definition of faith from the previous chapters, trusting in the Lord with all our heart is another way of expressing our wholehearted belief in God's promises to us. The alternative will only enslave us to the law of sin and death because our own understanding is corrupted by the knowledge of good and evil we inherited from Adam. By thinking of Him in all our ways, we continue to assert His Lordship in our lives. But how do we receive the guidance that is essential to our walk with Him, and how does He smooth our paths?

In the Old Testament, God spoke through "the word of the Lord" to individuals more than two hundred and fifty times. In the New Testament, God communicates with us through His Son Jesus Christ.

"My sheep hear my voice, and I know them,
and they follow me. I give them eternal life,
and they will never perish" (John 10:27, 28,
emphasis mine).

"My sheep *hear my voice* . . . and they follow me." The ability to perceive His voice enables us to follow Him. Jesus does not require a certain level of spirituality before we can recognize His voice. His only criteria: we must be His sheep. However, it takes time to become familiar enough with Him so we can identify His voice whenever He speaks to us. In fact, you may be hearing His voice but not recognizing it (see 1 Samuel 3:4-14).

> *"My sheep hear my voice . . . and they follow me."*
> *The ability to perceive His voice enables us to*
> *follow Him. Jesus does not require a certain level of*
> *spirituality before we can recognize His voice. His*
> *only criteria: we must be His sheep.*

Let's take a closer look at "the word of the Lord" where it is first revealed: in Genesis 15:1-4 (*emphasis mine*).

After these things the word of the Lord came
to Abram in a vision: "Fear not, Abram. I am
your shield; your reward shall be very great."
But Abram said, "O Lord God, what will you
give me, for I continue childless, and the heir
of my house is Eliezer of Damascus." . . . And
behold, the word of the Lord came to him:
"This man shall not be your heir; your very
own son shall be your heir."

Word is singular even though the Lord shared more than

one word with Abram. In other passages where this phrase is found, the "word" is anywhere from a sentence or two to dozens of sentences (See Jeremiah 2:1–3:5).

In addition, "the word of the Lord" *came* to Abram and Jeremiah. This may seem to be a rather odd way of describing an audible message. Even though Jesus said "My sheep *hear* my voice," we should not automatically assume we will *perceive* His voice exactly as we would when another person speaks to us. God is Spirit and everyone who worships Him must do so in spirit and in truth (John 4:24).

Furthermore, Jesus told His disciples at the Last Supper:

> "When the Spirit of truth comes, he will guide you into all the truth, for he will not speak on his own authority, but <u>whatever he hears he will speak</u>, and will declare to you the things that are to come" (John 16:13, *emphasis mine*).

We can conclude the Spirit relates to us what He receives—God's Spirit to our spirit—and declares to us the things that are to come. Our "ears to hear"[2] are the ears of our spirit, not our physical ears.

When the word of the Lord comes to me, it is like His knowledge or insight suddenly becomes apparent. I know it is from God because it is always accompanied by calmness and a conviction of its truthfulness.[3] He shares a revelation in a similar way that information is displayed on a computer screen. His wisdom does not come into my mind in a serial fashion like it would if it were spoken—it is just there all at once.

* * * * *

Personal Testimonies

Miriam graduated with a BA in piano performance from Alaska Methodist University in Anchorage. Because her senior recital in January was part of the paid civic-university concert series, there was extra pressure to perform at a professional level.

The program included well over a hundred pages of new music that had to be memorized that school year. In order to prepare adequately, she performed for several groups in early January.

Schumann's G minor Sonata No. 2, Op. 22 was one of the performance pieces, and Miriam could not play through one section on the third page of the last movement without stopping. She was terrified she might stumble during her concert.

The night of the performance, all went well until she began playing the Schumann. As she approached the dreaded passage, she became more frightened she would have to stop. At that moment, the Lord spoke to her, saying, "Relax, I'll play it for you." So, she emptied her mind and sailed right through the third page! No one in the audience knew.

At the conclusion of the concert, Miriam thanked her parents and teachers. Then, she thanked the Lord Jesus Christ for helping her.

* * *

Miriam and I started dating after I committed my life to Christ, and we attended the First Presbyterian Church in Anchorage, where she was a member. After graduation, we both got summer jobs. She was employed as the receptionist at church, and I worked as a flagman on a crew resurfacing the Glenn Highway from Palmer to the Alaskan border. Summer days are long in Alaska and our construction job meant that we labored twelve-hour days for six days a week.

One Tuesday morning in June, my flag station was at the bridge over Moose Creek about six and a half miles from Palmer. It had started to rain and I didn't think anything about it until the driver of the escort car piloting traffic through the construction site mentioned it only seemed to be raining right at the bridge. Looking back along the string of stopped vehicles, I could see windshield wipers were on only on those cars near the bridge.

That rain was my "burning bush" encounter, for as soon as the line of cars had left and I had stopped the next queue of traffic, the Lord spoke to me: "Pick up a stone from the river bank and try to clean it." I did, and He continued: "Now, drop the rock in the stream." After a few moments, He said, "Retrieve it and you will see your best efforts could not match how clean the stone is now. No matter how much a person tries to purify their life, their attempts can't compare to the cleansing of my River of Life.

"Look at the cottonwood trees lining the bank. They are much taller and healthier because they send their roots deep into the moist soil. Stay close to Me and plant your roots deep into my soil for I am calling you to lead others to my River of Life in Jesus Christ."

I glanced at my watch—it was 10 a.m.

That evening at home in Palmer, I wrote a letter to our minister telling him the Lord had called me to lead others to Jesus Christ, and I wanted to discuss this with him after the Sunday service. I also asked him not to share this information with Miriam because I wanted to tell her myself.

Sunday, after I picked her up and we were on our way to church, she asked me if the Lord had called me to be a minister. Surprised, I thought, *Our pastor just couldn't keep a secret*. I was even more amazed when she told me how she knew.

"Tuesday is my day off," she said. "That morning about 10 a.m., I was having tea with my mother and I said to her, 'I think God is calling Bill into the ministry.'"

＊ ＊ ＊

Linda, one of the elders of our church in Montesano, Washington, was diagnosed with ovarian cancer. During surgery, the doctor removed both ovaries, her uterus, and her fallopian tubes. After the operation in Aberdeen, the doctor told her husband he had never seen a more aggressive case. In fact, he was sending samples to Seattle for further analysis. The results would be back in a week. In the meantime, Linda could go home after her recovery in the hospital.

Several days later, I noticed Linda's husband walking up the sidewalk toward our house. Miriam saw him too, and from the kitchen she said, "The tumors went up malignant but they came back benign." He knocked at our door and when I opened it, his face was beaming. "The Seattle lab said Linda does not have cancer! The results of their tests were all benign."

* * *

My sister Valerie suffered most of her life with bloating, weight loss, and vomiting. She received treatment both in Anchorage and Seattle and was told the condition was largely in her head.

Three years ago, the Lord told me she had celiac disease. I encouraged her to remove gluten from her diet for a month and see if her condition improved.

Four days later, she called to tell me her appetite had returned. During the next month, her other medical problems began to recover—especially the vomiting. Her doctor, however, dismissed her explanation, saying a change of mood had triggered her reduction in symptoms.

Recently, however, after her latest colonoscopy and the removal of a polyp, another physician said the tests revealed she had celiac disease. He recommended she remove gluten from her diet.

＊ ＊ ＊ ＊ ＊

I share these experiences with you to highlight the fact God still communicates with us today just like He did in biblical times. Miriam and I could not have received this level of guidance by meditating on the Scriptures. The word of the Lord is an essential component of our walk with Him.

God's Peace

The word of the Lord, however, is rarely a daily occurrence. The third component is God's peace. As soon as Isaac was old enough to marry, Abraham sent his most trusted servant to his relatives in the city of Nahor in Mesopotamia to find a mate for his son.

God previously told Abraham his progeny would be descendants of Isaac (Genesis 21:12). Believing the Lord would bless his efforts to obtain a suitable spouse, he commissioned his servant.

> "The Lord, the God of heaven, who took me from my father's house and from the land of my kindred, and who spoke to me and swore to me, 'To your offspring I will give this land,' he will send his angel before you, and you shall take a wife for my son from there" (Genesis 24:7).

There is no indication the angel communicated with his servant during his journey. Yet, when he found Rebekah and her family, he immediately knew what to say to them.

> "Blessed be the Lord, the God of my master Abraham, who has not forsaken his steadfast love and his faithfulness toward my master. As for me, <u>the Lord has led me in the way</u> to the house of my master's kinsmen" (Genesis 24:27, *emphasis mine*).

How did the servant know God was leading him *in the way*? Jesus provides an answer with these words to His disciples.

> "But the Helper, the Holy Spirit, whom the Father will send in my name, he will teach you all things and bring to your remembrance all that I have said to you. <u>Peace I leave with you; my peace I give to you. Not as the world gives do I give to you. Let not your hearts be troubled, neither let them be afraid</u>" (John 14:26, 27, *emphasis mine*).

His disciples would face many daunting challenges in the months and years ahead. Some of these new obstacles would be terrifying and work to dissuade them from preaching the Gospel. Even though the Holy Spirit would bring to their remembrance all that Jesus had said to them, those words said in earlier contexts might do little to assist them in their present situation. So Christ gave them His peace to quell their troubled hearts. How would His peace overcome their fears?

Paul also faced seemingly insurmountable hurdles, and experienced firsthand the Lord's peace.

> The Lord is at hand; do not be anxious about anything, but in everything by prayer and supplication with thanksgiving let your requests be made known to God. And the peace of God, which surpasses all understanding, will guard your hearts and your minds in Christ Jesus (Philippians 4:5-7).

Paul assures us we do not need to worry about anything because the Lord is with us *in the circumstance we are facing.* Instead of being anxious, he encourages us to present our requests to God by prayer and humble petition with thanksgiving. If we do, the peace of God—the same peace Christ promised His disciples—will guard[4] our hearts and minds in Christ Jesus.

The peace of God, one of the fruits of the Spirit (Galatians 5:22, 23), is "not as the world gives." It surpasses all understanding because normal peace departs when times are traumatic.

Anxiety is a signal we do not have a solution for a given situation. Worry can also result from our repeated attempts to figure out a remedy on our own.

Christ's peace is like the referee in a team sport who blows his whistle only when a participant goes out of bounds or executes a maneuver not allowed by the rules. The umpire is the guardian or protector of the game's conduct.

As long as we are "walking in the way," Christ's peace remains in our hearts and minds, guarding and protecting us from the worry and anxiety normally accompanying a stressful environment. If His peace leaves us and we begin to feel anxious about the next steps to take, we should avoid our innate tendency to solve the problem ourselves. Instead, He will restore His peace if we bring our requests to Him through prayer, realizing that, thankfully, He is there with us.

> *Christ's peace is like the referee in a team sport who blows his whistle only when a participant goes out of bounds or executes a maneuver not allowed by the rules. The umpire is the guardian or protector of the game's conduct.*

Back to Abraham's servant. This man knew how to travel to the city of Nahor in Mesopotamia. He understood the customs of the region expected women to fetch water for their families. Those same traditions also required residents to offer hospitality to strangers.[5] So, if he stayed by the well, he would surely meet women who would be hospitable to him.

He did not know how to find Abraham's kinsmen or which one would be God's choice for Isaac. But instead of spending the day at the well asking questions of everyone who came, he made this request to the Lord.

> "O Lord, God of my master Abraham, please grant me success today and show steadfast love to my master Abraham. Behold, I am standing by the spring of water, and the daughters of the men of the city are coming out to draw water. Let the young woman to whom I shall say, 'Please let down your jar that I may drink,' and who shall say, 'Drink, and I will water your camels' — let her be the one whom you have appointed for your servant Isaac. By this I shall know that you have shown steadfast love to my master" (Genesis 24:12-14).

He did not know how to find Abraham's kinsmen or which one would be God's choice for Isaac.

The servant had just finished praying when Rebekah came from the well with a jar of water on her shoulder. When he asked her for a drink, she replied she would also water his

camels—a huge task since each of his ten camels could consume as much as thirty gallons![6]

There is no indication Rebekah was asking the Lord for
anything special that day. She was only doing what she had
done nearly every day. To the casual observer, she *happened to
pass by Abraham's servant at the precise moment he concluded
his prayer.* To the servant, his request and her response assured
him she had been chosen by God for Isaac. The peace of God,
precipitated by this answer to his prayer, enabled him to say,
"As for me, the Lord has led me *in the way* to the house of my
master's kinsmen." In like manner, the Lord utilizes His peace
to counsel us as we walk *in the way.*

Suffering

> From that time Jesus began to show his disci-
> ples that he must go to Jerusalem and suffer
> many things from the elders and chief priests
> and scribes, and be killed, and on the third
> day be raised. And Peter took him aside and
> began to rebuke him, saying, "Far be it from
> you, Lord. This shall never happen to you."
> But he turned and said to Peter, "Get behind
> me, Satan! You are a hindrance to me. For
> you are not setting your mind on the things
> of God, but on the things of man" (Matthew
> 16:21-23, *emphasis mine*).

No one likes to suffer[7] because, like Peter, we do not view
it as beneficial to our walk in the way. This mindset only high-

lights our reliance on the knowledge of good and evil we inherited from Adam.

One reason Christ offers us His peace is to counter the persecution we will face for our allegiance to Him. Without its assurance, our natural inclination will be to abandon the Gospel to avoid suffering.

> For it has been granted to you that for the sake of Christ you should not only believe in him but also suffer for his sake, engaging in the same conflict that you saw I had and now hear that I still have (Philippians 1:29, 30).

> Indeed, all who desire to live a godly life in Christ Jesus will be persecuted" (2 Timothy 3:12).

After his encounter with Christ on the road to Damascus left him temporarily blind, Paul was taken to a house in the city. The Lord appeared to Ananias in a vision.

> "Rise and go to a street called Straight, and at the house of Judas look for a man of Tarsus named Saul, for behold, he is praying, and he has seen in a vision a man named Ananias come in and lay his hands on him so that he might regain his sight. . . . Go, for he is a chosen instrument of mine to carry my name before the Gentiles and kings and the children of Israel. For I will show him how much he must suffer for the sake of my name" (Acts 9:11-16, *emphasis mine*).

I have always admired the depth of knowledge and wisdom Paul shares with us through his letters. He did not acquire this comprehension in rabbinical school. It was forged in the crucible of his experience and adversity.

A cursory look at 2 Corinthians 11:16-12:10 shows the extent of Paul's tumultuous "walk in the way." He was even stoned (Acts 14:19, 20)! Paul ends this litany in 2 Corinthians with an account of a man who was caught up into paradise and heard things that cannot be told and may not be uttered. Because his near-death experience was so incredibly profound, he wrote:

> A thorn was given me in the flesh, a messenger from Satan to harass me, to keep me from becoming conceited. Three times I pleaded with the Lord about this, that it should leave me. But he said to me, "My grace is sufficient for you, <u>for my power is made perfect in weakness</u>." Therefore, I will boast all the more gladly of my weaknesses, so that the power of Christ may rest upon me. <u>For the sake of Christ, then, I am content with weakness, insults, hardships, persecutions, and calamities. For when I am weak, then I am strong</u> (2 Corinthians 12:7-10, *emphasis mine*).

Paul begged three times to have this impediment removed because he wanted to present himself in the best possible light when he shared the gospel. But the Lord told Paul if he relied on his own natural strengths, he would hinder Christ living within him from manifesting *His power*.

This is a hard lesson to learn because when we share our faults and weaknesses we are likely to feel naked and open to ridicule, scorn, and even persecution. But by doing so, people can more easily relate to us as flawed human beings who are more—not less—like them. This allows the Holy Spirit to spotlight areas where *they* are naked and to increase their aspirations to clothe themselves with Christ's righteousness.

> *The Lord told Paul if he relied on his own natural strengths, he would hinder Christ living within him from manifesting* His power.

James shares another benefit when we encounter different types of trials.

> Count it all joy, my brothers, when you meet trials of various kinds, for you know that the testing of your faith produces steadfastness. And let steadfastness have its full effect, that you may be perfect and complete, lacking in nothing (James 1:2-4, *emphasis mine*).

Another word for steadfastness is fortitude, and the discipline gained from the trials we face that test our faith yields fortitude. The goal of this discipline molds our character to become more resilient, courageous, and skilled in every aspect of life.

Walking in the Way

> Have this mind among yourselves, which is yours in Christ Jesus, who, though he was in the form of God, did not count equality with God a thing to be grasped, but emptied himself, by taking the form of a servant, being born in the likeness of men. And being found

in human form, <u>he humbled himself</u> by becoming obedient to the point of death, even death on a cross. Therefore, God has highly exalted him and bestowed on him the name that is above every name . . . Therefore, my beloved, as you have always obeyed, so now not only as in my presence but much more in my absence, <u>work out your own salvation with fear and trembling, for it is God who works in you, both to will and to work for his good pleasure</u>. Do all things without grumbling or disputing, that you may be blameless and innocent, children of God without blemish in the midst of a crooked and twisted generation, <u>among whom you shine as lights in the world</u> (Philippians 2:5-15, *emphasis mine*).

Jesus is our example for how to walk in the way. Paul reminded the Philippians that Christ did not crave any selfish ambition but humbled Himself even to death on the cross and was highly exalted by His Father for successfully completing His role in salvation history. Paul asked those reading his letter to follow Christ's example and work out their own salvation roles—their own walk in the way—in fear and trembling. They would not achieve this on their own. God would be performing the actual work in them, giving them both the will and the ability to fulfill His good pleasure.

A quick look at Noah's part in God's plan will allow us to better understand why Paul added the phrase "in fear and trembling." Noah was a righteous man in a corrupt and wicked generation. The Lord asked him to build an ark 300 cubits long, 50 cubits wide, and 30 cubits high. If we convert those measurements to feet, this barge was 450 by 75 by 45 feet—one and a half times the length of a football field!

Made of hewn wood, it likely took years to complete and was so enormous, it could only be assembled out in the open in full view of everyone. It is not difficult to imagine the taunts, mockery, and threats Noah and his family constantly received from those who lived nearby.

How could he maintain his focus in the face of continuous insults year after year? Answer: he walked with God (Genesis 6:9).

> The fear of the Lord is the beginning of wisdom, and the knowledge of the Holy One is insight (Proverbs 9:10).

The fear of the Lord is the *beginning* of wisdom—a reverential fear that allowed Noah to know the God he worshiped was able to accomplish everything He revealed including bringing a flood large enough to destroy all the earth's inhabitants.

What would have happened if Noah stopped building the ark for fear of what his neighbors might do to him and his family? His walk with the Holy One gave him the peace and assurance to literally work out his own salvation in fear and trembling.

In addition, the Lord gave Noah the insight to appreciate how his blameless and innocent life shone as a light in the midst of his crooked and twisted generation (to paraphrase Philippians 2:15).

> *What would have happened if Noah stopped building the ark for fear of what his neighbors might do to him and his family?*

Paul advises us to follow Christ's example not to seek any selfish ambition that would deter us from the unique blueprint God is revealing to each of us as we walk with Him. If we humble ourselves, He will give us both the desire and the ability to implement His good pleasure. He will also establish us as beacons of light in our world so desperately in need of His salvation.

It is my prayer you will experience all three ways the Lord leads us so that you may be more effectively led by the Spirit as you walk in the way.

Study Questions for Discussion

- Why is the Bible the foundation for understanding our relationship with God (Joshua 1:5-9; 2 Timothy 3:15-17)?

  - Why is it not the only source of guidance for believers (Psalm 119:105)?

- Why is it important for us to be able to recognize God's voice (John 10:27, 28)?

  - Are our "ears to hear" the word of the Lord our physical ears or the ears of our spirit (Genesis 15:1-4; Matthew 11:15, 13:9, 43; Revelation 2:7)?

- The "word of the Lord" is rarely a daily occurrence. How does the peace of God guide us as we walk in the way (Genesis 24:27; John 14:26, 27; Philippians 4:5-7)?

  - What roles do worry and anxiety play as we walk in the way?

  - Why is God's peace so important when we suffer (Acts 9:11-16; Philippians 1:29, 30; 2 Timothy 3:12)?

- How can we be strong when we are weak (2 Corinthians 12:7-10)?
  - Does it help others to more easily relate to us?
- Is there a benefit to us when we encounter different types of trials (James 1:2-4)?
- How is Christ our example for walking in the way (Philippians 2:5-15)?
  - How does the fear of the Lord help us walk in the way (Proverbs 9:10)?
    - How is our walk a witness to others?

Eight
We Do Not Wrestle
Against Flesh and Blood

Finally, be strong in the Lord and in the strength of his might. Put on the whole armor of God, <u>that you may be able to stand against the schemes of the devil. For we do not wrestle against flesh and blood</u>, but against rulers, against the authorities, against the cosmic powers over this present darkness, against the spiritual forces of evil in the heavenly places. Therefore, take up the whole armor of God, that you may be able to withstand in the evil day, and having done all, to stand firm (Ephesians 6:10-13, *emphasis mine*).

The Other Adversary

Part of the reason we face persecution when we share our commitment to Christ is that Satan, the prince of this world, is behind much of the oppression. I say this because it is easy to focus on the individuals resisting us instead of the spirit at work inspiring them.

And you were dead in the trespasses and sins in which you once walked, following the course of this world, following the prince of the power of the air, <u>the spirit that is now at work in the sons of disobedience</u> (Ephesians 2:1, 2, *emphasis mine*).

My counsel for dealing with this other adversary can best be found in the following texts.

Be sober-minded; be watchful. Your adversary the devil prowls around like a roaring lion, seeking someone to devour. <u>Resist him, firm in your faith, knowing that the same kinds of suffering are being experienced by your brotherhood throughout the world</u> (1 Peter 5:8, 9 *emphasis mine*).

Submit yourselves therefore to God. <u>Resist the devil, and he will flee from you</u> (James 4:7, *emphasis mine*).

Little children, you are from God and have overcome them, for <u>he who is in you is greater than he who is in the world</u> (1 John 4:4, *emphasis mine*).

I also offer you the advice of a wise Christian friend who once told me, "Don't try to drive the darkness out—just turn on the Light." I won't attempt to "drive the darkness out" by devoting numerous pages to this subject. As an alternative, I will finish this chapter with some personal encounters.

> *Don't try to drive the darkness out—just turn on the Light.*

* * * * *

Personal Testimonies

Satan and his minions often harassed my wife and me shortly after I was ordained and began serving the Lord as a pastor. They usually pestered us Saturday night when I needed a good night's rest. Their technique: a constant pounding on the walls and hands descending from the ceiling. These disturbances kept us awake most of the night. When we did get to sleep, Miriam was often awakened by my restlessness. Turning, she could see me wrestling with a dark figure hovering over my body, and she rebuked it.

Even though we dispelled these evil spirits, relief from them didn't last long before the commotion returned. That is . . . until we detected a pattern to their harassment. Every Sunday following their attempts to keep us awake was a true blessing. People either committed their lives to Christ or attended our services for the first time and wanted to be part of our congregation.

Once we recognized their behavior, we knew our unwelcome visitors had somehow learned of Sunday's upcoming events and were orchestrating these pranks to interrupt our sleep. The next time the hassles began, we sat up in bed, thanked them for letting us know the worship service would be special, and told them it didn't matter if they badgered us all night.

Like mischievous children caught in the act, the troublemaking stopped.

* * *

One afternoon while I was at the church office, Miriam decided to open our front door for no apparent reason. When she did, there stood Satan as a handsome young man dressed in black. Although he glanced occasionally at her face, she noticed right away his eyes never met hers. She was not afraid and chided, "You poor, miserable creature! You can't even look me in the eye!"

As soon as Miriam said this, it was as if a giant hand pushed him, and he fell back onto the ground, which opened up beneath him. As she looked on, the earth swallowed him up.

* * *

One night after working on chapter 7 of this book, I crawled into bed and reached to turn out the light.

Suddenly, everything went black and I was enveloped by a huge dark form that coiled around me like a serpent. It squeezed so tight I couldn't breathe, and I felt a rod about the size of a walking stick being thrust into my back.

I could tell it was trying to kill me because the harder I struggled, the more it tightened its coils and shoved the shaft into my back. So I called out, "I rebuke you in the name of Jesus Christ! Leave me and my wife alone."

The menacing force left immediately, and I thanked the Lord for His protection.

Study Questions for Discussion

- Paul tells us to put on the whole armor of God that we may be able to stand against the schemes of the devil. Is this stance a defensive or an offensive posture (Ephesians 6:10-13)?

  - How does Ephesians 6:13-18 support your conclusion?

  - Why is it important to recognize we do not war against flesh and blood when we face trials and persecution from others (Ephesians 2:1, 2)?

- Satan loves attention. Are we focusing on him when we try offensively to "drive the darkness out?"

- Satan is a formidable adversary (Job 1:6-2:10). If he is so powerful and worthy of our respect, why should we not fear him (John 16:33; James 4:7; 1 John 4:4)?

- Why is turning on the light of the Gospel God's way of defeating Satan (Luke 10:1, 2, 9, 17-20)?

Nine
Living in God's Rest

> Thus the heavens and the earth were finished,
> and all the host of them. And on the seventh
> day God finished his work that he had done,
> and he rested on the seventh day from all his
> work that he had done. So God blessed the
> seventh day and made it holy, because on it
> God rested from all his work that he had done
> in creation (Genesis 2:1-3).

This familiar text says God finished creation in six days

and rested on the seventh. He then blessed the seventh day

and later enshrined it in the Ten Commandments as a day to

rest from one's labors and as a holy day for worship (Exodus

20:8-11; 31:12-17).

God's Rest for Moses

But there is more to God's rest than setting aside a day to

refrain from work to worship Him.

> Moses said to the Lord, "See, you say to me,
> 'Bring up this people,' but you have not let me
> know whom you will send with me. Yet you
> have said, 'I know you by name, and you have
> also found favor in my sight.' Now therefore,
> if I have found favor in your sight, please show
> me now your ways, that I may know you in
> order to find favor in your sight. Consider too
> that this nation is your people." And he said,
> "My presence will go with you, and I will give
> you rest" (Exodus 33:12-14, *emphasis mine*).

It's easy to tell that Moses was frustrated with "this nation [of] your people." He appreciated knowing he had found favor with God. But he desperately needed someone to go with him to show him the Lord's way of coping. God promised He would always be available in the midst of every exasperating situation. And to calm his harried mind, God said he would give Moses *rest*.

Clearly, He was not suggesting an extra day off or a vacation to get away for a while. The Lord was offering His own rest. God is not fatigued or wearied the way we are (Isaiah 40:28). So, His rest had to be associated with a posture or mindset Moses could adopt to deal with the interminable circumstances the two of them would face with this generation of Israelites.

God had delivered them from Egypt with unprecedented displays of power. But they would shortly refuse to believe He could help them successfully enter and possess the land promised to Abraham. Psalm 95:7-11 indicates they continually went astray and would not learn His ways and, as a result, God swore they would never achieve His rest.

> *Clearly, He was not suggesting an extra day off or a vacation to get away for a while. The Lord was offering His own* rest.

Those who resided in Canaan could not possibly present

as significant a challenge to the Lord as the legions of Pharaoh. So the people were, essentially, *faithless*. Let's consider the circumstances surrounding their rejection of God's leadership to better understand why the Israelites never gained access to His rest.

No Rest for the Israelites

Before the Lord asked Moses to lead the children of Israel into Canaan, He asked him to send twelve spies to inspect the region and return with a report. Here is a look at this incursion through the eyes of the inhabitants.

* * * * *

The territory between Egypt and Canaan was camel country. Merchant caravans regularly plied trade routes to and from Egypt that serviced the larger, well-fortified Canaanite cities (Exodus 13:28).

According to Numbers 1:1-46, Moses counted all males twenty years old and up who could go to war. His tally added to 603,550 men. Since Moses did not count women, children, and men not able to fight, the number of Israelites in the wilderness likely totaled well over a million.

This gigantic population, moving slowly across

the landscape, would be quite noticeable to anyone traveling in the region. Their voluminous presence would also be an unusual occurrence and the subject of conversation among the caravans' trading partners.

Furthermore, it is not hard to imagine at least some of these merchants asking the Israelites about their destination. The observations they gleaned from these encounters would be shared with their customers in Canaan especially once they realized the Israelites wanted to occupy this very same territory their God had promised to their forefathers.

Here is some of the information that might have been disclosed to the Canaanites.

- The Israelites had been slaves in Egypt and their God delivered them from lifelong servitude through many miracles including killing all the firstborn children in Egypt from Pharaoh's house on down;

- Their God saved them from an Egyptian battalion tasked with bringing them back. He did so by parting the Red Sea so they could cross over on dry ground. When the Egyptian troops tried to follow, their God drowned them by closing the ocean over them;

- Their God had promised their ancestors an inheritance occupied at that time by the Canaanites, Hittites, Amorites, Perizzites, Hivites, and Jebusites;

- They camped for some time at Mount Sinai where their God gave them His laws. He also descended on the mountaintop in fire accompanied by thunder, lightning, and thick clouds like the smoke from a kiln;

- Their God fed them in the wilderness. Each day for six days every week, He covered the ground with manna that tasted like wafers made with honey. The people gathered this food for each day's meal and, strangely, on the sixth day, He provided enough for the next two days;

- Whenever they stayed in a place with no water, their leader struck a rock with his staff and their God brought forth a spring of water for the people and animals to drink;

- When the Israelites moved from encampment to encampment, their God led them in a pillar of a cloud by day and a pillar of fire by night;
- This multitude was now stationed in the wilderness of Paran near their southern frontier. They could deploy more than six hundred thousand soldiers and had just sent twelve spies across the border into Canaan.

Even though they lived in large, well-fortified cities, their inhabitants also possessed the knowledge of good and evil. The residents compared their strengths and weaknesses with those of the Israelites they had heard about from the merchants. The sons of the Anakim comprised a small portion of their population, men both large and tall with a formidable reputation: "Who can stand before the sons of Anak?" (Deuteronomy 9:1-3).

Unfortunately, the descendants of Anak would be no match against more than six hundred thousand soldiers and their God who had delivered them from Pharaoh and his armies! The Canaanite gods never demonstrated anything comparable to the Israelites' God. If He promised their forefathers this property, the current occupants would stand little chance against a direct assault.

They could kill the spies. But that would only infuriate the conquering hoard. So, they hatched a plan. Perhaps they could intimidate the spies and thereby dissuade the Israelites from invading. If the spies only encountered the Anakim during their expedition, they might be frightened by the prospect of meeting them in battle. (For comparison, Goliath's height was six cubits and a span, which translates to ten and a half feet tall; 1 Samuel 17:4.[1] He may have been a remnant of the giants defeated by the Ammonites (Deuteronomy 2:20, 21)). In any event, the children of Anak towered over the spies.

> *So, they hatched a plan. Perhaps they could intimidate the spies and thereby dissuade the Israelites from invading.*

One final component of their strategy: as soon as the scouts returned, they would station their most seasoned troops on the border to repel any invasion as best they could.

Their plan worked. When the spies returned, their report was mixed. Joshua and Caleb said the country was flowing with milk and honey. They even brought a cluster of grapes and some pomegranates and figs with them and concluded by saying the Lord would deliver the Canaanites into their hands.

But the other spies lamented about large and well-fortified cities and a territory that would devour them.

> "All the people that we saw were of great height. And there we saw the Nephilim (the sons of Anak, who come from the Nephilim), and we seemed to ourselves like grasshoppers, and so we seemed to them" (Numbers 13:32, 33, *emphasis mine*).

The Israelites also possessed the knowledge of good and evil. They had been slaves in Egypt, not warriors. Comparing their combat abilities with those of the residents, supposing *all of them were of great height*, they determined they would be slaughtered if they tried to invade. So they trusted their own understanding instead of the Lord's ability to overcome any obstacle.

When a small contingent did invade after the Lord said He would not be with them, the Canaanites soundly defeated them.

* * * * *

God's Rest for Us Who Believe

The writer of Hebrews begins by quoting Psalm 95:7-11 to more comprehensibly define God's rest. He also explains how the Israelites failed to appropriate His rest and how it is available to us who believe.

> Today, <u>if you hear his voice</u>, do not harden your hearts as in the rebellion, on the day of testing in the wilderness. . . . "They always go astray in their heart; they have not known my ways. As I swore in my wrath, '<u>They shall not enter my rest</u>.'"
>
> . . . <u>To whom did he swear that they would not enter his rest</u>, but to those who were disobedient? So we see that they <u>were unable to enter because of unbelief.</u>
>
> . . . For <u>good news</u> came to us just as to them. . . . <u>We who have believed enter that rest</u>, as he has said, "I swore in my wrath, 'They shall not enter my rest,'" <u>although his works were finished from the foundation of the world.</u>
>
> . . . If Joshua had given them rest, God would not have spoken of another day later on. So then, there remains a Sabbath rest for the people of God, <u>for whoever has entered God's rest has also rested from his works as God did from his</u>. Let us therefore <u>strive to enter that rest</u>, so that no one may fall by the same sort of disobedience (Hebrews 3:7-4:11, *emphasis mine*).

These brief segments[2] focus on God's rest. They indicate

those who rebelled did not obtain His rest because of their unbelief. So, faith is a requirement for entry.

In addition, *we who have believed* in the good news of the gospel *enter* that rest. The word *enter* is a present tense verb and is so important it begins the third verse in the Greek text. As such, it indicates entering His rest is not a one-time event but a *continual* posture of faith. *Have believed* is a past tense participle, meaning our acceptance of Jesus Christ as our Lord and Savior enables us to participate in God's rest.

Finished from the Foundation of the World

The word *although* links our entry into His rest with the works He "finished from the foundation of the world," making it clear the tasks He rested from in Genesis 2:2, 3 include much more than what He accomplished in creation. There are a number of New Testament passages proclaiming the extent of His achievements.

> I have been crucified with Christ (Galatians 2:20).

> But God, being rich in mercy, because of the great love with which he loved us, even when we were dead in our trespasses, <u>made us alive together with Christ</u>—by grace you have been saved—and <u>raised us up with him</u> and <u>seated us with him</u> in the heavenly places in Christ Jesus (Ephesians 2:4-6, *emphasis mine*).

And all who dwell on earth will worship it
[the beast], everyone <u>whose name has not</u>
<u>been written before the foundation of the</u>
<u>world in the book of life of the Lamb who was</u>
<u>slain</u> (Revelation 13:9, *emphasis mine*).

Through faith, we were crucified, raised up, and seated in the heavenly places *together* with Christ. Even though Paul and the rest of us were not present when Christ was crucified, God incorporated our death into His death and raised us up and seated us *with Him* at His own right hand (Ephesians 1:20). Since Abraham beheld Christ's day and was glad, he too participated in Christ's death and resurrection.

Every believer's name was written in the Lamb's book of life before the dawn of creation. So God completed the entire scope of salvation history through His Son Jesus Christ *before* the world began.

> *Even though Paul and the rest of us were not present when Christ was crucified, God incorporated our death into His death and raised us up and seated us with Him at His own right hand (Ephesians 1:20).*

The last segment from Hebrews defines the Sabbath rest available for the people of God. The phrase "whoever has entered God's rest" refers to the previous segment "we who have believed enter that rest." The word *rested* (Hebrews 4:10) is a past tense verb, meaning we can adopt a posture of rest from our work because it is already finished in the same way God has rested from His completed work.

God's Posture of Rest

The previous segment said God viewed all of His accomplishments throughout history as completed "from the foundation of the world." How can the Lord adopt this posture? The Lord not only knows what will occur as history progresses from creation through the manifestation of the new heavens and the new earth. He is also an active participant in that history.

> For <u>we are his workmanship</u>, created in Christ Jesus for good works, <u>which God prepared beforehand, that we should walk in them</u> (Ephesians 2:10, *emphasis mine*).

> And we know that for those who love God all things work together for good, for those who are called according to his purpose. For <u>those whom he foreknew</u> he also <u>predestined</u> to be conformed to the image of his Son, in order that he might be the firstborn among many brothers. And <u>those whom he predestined</u> he also <u>called</u>, and <u>those whom he called</u> he also <u>justified</u>, and <u>those whom he justified</u> he also <u>glorified</u> (Romans 8:28-30, *emphasis mine*).

Every verb describing God's activity in these two passages is in the past tense! Because He is eternal and not bound by time, everything He achieves within His timeless dimension of eternity is also *completed* within the framework of time.[3]

Our Posture of Rest

Since acquiring His rest is achieved through our posture of faith and not as a privilege granted when we became Christians, the writer of Hebrews challenges us to "strive to enter that rest." As long as we think the entry into *our* promised land is somehow dependent upon what *we* must accomplish, we will be turned back by the "Anakim" standing in our way. Instead, we can recognize, through faith, that the tasks God is calling us to achieve have already been completed for us beforehand, enabling us to rest in the finished work of Christ.

An Example of Rest

Let's say you go to a baseball game and, in the ninth inning, the visiting team is ahead by one run. With the tying run on at first base and two outs, the batter works the pitcher to a full count: three balls and two strikes. The crowd holds its collective breath as the pitcher hurls a fastball down the middle of the strike zone—only to erupt in thunderous shouting as the batter connects for a home run to win the game.

You leave the stadium still pumped up from the results of that final at bat. The next evening, you watch the sports report on the six o'clock news to savor the moment one last time.

Once again, the count is full with two outs and a runner on at first base. This time, however, your heart is not in your throat as you watch the opposing pitcher wind up to throw. Why? Because you know what will happen next. Instead of being anxious, you can *rest* in the knowledge the batter will deliver a home run to win the game.

Likewise, we can rest knowing the outcome of the events God calls us to participate in is *assured,* just as remembering the final at bat at the ballpark allows us to rest while watching the replay on the next day's news.

This is why without faith it is impossible to please Him (Hebrews 11:6). His ways are higher than our ways and His thoughts are higher than our thoughts (Isaiah 55:8). We are unable to accomplish anything for God on our own (John 15:5) because everything we do based on our own understanding lies outside His finished work.

> "Not everyone who says to me, 'Lord, Lord,' will enter the kingdom of heaven, but the one who does the will of my Father who is in heaven. On that day many will say to me, 'Lord, Lord, did we not prophesy in your name, and cast out demons in your name, and do many mighty works in your name?' And then will I declare to them, 'I never knew you; depart from me, you workers of lawlessness'" (Matthew 7:21-23, *emphasis mine*).

From a human perspective, these folks are doing God's

work and are very religious. There is only one problem. There is no personal relationship with the God they are trying to serve. Jesus declares "I never knew you" and commands them to leave His presence. He says they are "workers of lawlessness" precisely because everything they are doing is governed by the law of sin and death rather than by the law of the Spirit of Life. In other words, they cannot please the Lord because there is nothing they are accomplishing that is part of His salvation history completed before the earth was formed.

> *We are unable to accomplish anything for God on our own (John 15:5) because everything we do based on our own understanding lies outside His finished work.*

Jesus Is Our Rest

> So Jesus said to them, "Truly, truly, I say to you, the Son can do nothing of his own accord, but only what he sees the Father doing. For whatever the Father does, that the Son does likewise. For the Father loves the Son and shows him all that he himself is doing" (John 5:19, 20).

There is more to this passage than a reply to His detractors. Jesus later told His disciples both He and His Father would make their home with those who love Him (John 14:23). His relationship with His Father remains the same. That is, Jesus is still only doing what He observes His Father doing and the Father, who loves the Son, continues to show Him all his finished work. Only now, Jesus does what He detects His Father doing *in and through us.* How? Through His body, the church.

> Now you are <u>the body of Christ and individually members of it</u>. And God has appointed in the church first apostles, second prophets, third teachers, then miracles, then gifts of healing, helping, administrating, and various kinds of tongues. . . . Earnestly desire the higher gifts (1 Corinthians 12:27-31, *emphasis mine*).

We are members of the body of Christ with Him as our head (Ephesians 1:22, 23). The individual organs of our own body work together in harmony. In like manner, we are equipped with unique spiritual gifts functioning under His guidance as our Head and in the power and wisdom of the Spirit (John 16:13). This allows us to perform the finished work the Father continues to show His Son.[4]

> Now I rejoice in my sufferings for your sake, and in my flesh I am filling up what is lacking in Christ's afflictions for the sake of <u>his body</u>, that is, <u>the church</u>, of which I became a minister . . . to make the word of God fully known, the hidden mystery . . . now revealed to the saints . . . which is <u>Christ in you</u>, the hope of glory. Him we proclaim . . . that we may present everyone mature in Christ. For this I toil, struggling with all <u>his energy that he powerfully works within me</u> (Colossians 1:24-28, *emphasis mine*).

All the work the Father shows the Son was performed before the beginning of creation. We can enter God's rest through faith knowing His completed work is both revealed to us and carried out in us by Jesus Christ—with *all His energy* that He continues to manifest within us.

Study Questions for Discussion

- When God rested from all His work on the seventh day (Genesis 2:1-3), did His rest include more than His work in creation?

- What did God mean when He said to Moses, "I will give you rest" (Exodus 33:14)?

- Why were the Israelites unable to enter into God's rest (Hebrews 3:19)?

- How do we know that all of salvation history has been finished "from the foundation of the world" (Hebrews 4:3; Galatians 2:20; Ephesians 2:4-6; Revelation 13:9)?

- How do we enter into God's rest (Hebrews 4:6-10)?

    - What is your definition of God's rest?

    - Is entering God's rest a privilege granted to us when we became Christians?

- How can the Lord adopt His posture of rest (Ephesians 2:10; Romans 8:28-30)?

- How is Jesus our rest (Colossians 1:24-28)?

- How can we enter God's rest while we are actively engaged in the work He has called us to perform

(Hebrews 4:10, 11)?

- Why is it impossible to please God except through faith (Hebrews 11:6)?

Ten
Follow Me

Your Pursuit of the Truth

If you are like me, your pursuit of the truth is a big deal.
I said in chapter 7 that the Bible is one of three ways the Lord
reveals His truth to us. It forms the foundation for our knowledge of the relationship we have with God. So, it is essential we
know how to interpret the Bible[1].

> Do your best to present yourself to God as
> one approved, a worker who has no need to
> be ashamed, rightly handling the word of
> truth (2 Timothy 2:15).

"Rightly handling the word of truth" is not as straight-
forward as it might appear. Let's examine some areas that can
obscure our perspective.

Translation versus Original Language

Chances are you study the Bible using a translation. This
is understandable since we learn to read in our mother tongue.
Nevertheless, a one-to-one correlation between the language
you are reading and the primary version is not often possible.
Take for example a phrase from Genesis 3:15: ". . . he shall
bruise your head, and you shall bruise his heel." That render-

ing points to a particular son of Eve who would bruise the head of the serpent. But, as pointed out in chapter 2, the Hebrew can also be rendered as: ". . . they shall bruise your head and you shall bruise their heal." This translation focuses on the continuing conflict between Eve's progeny and Satan. Both are valid interpretations. But only one can be selected by the translators.

Just as phrases can be expressed in more than one way, each word can be translated by more than one term or phrase. Synonyms are similar but not identical. So, it is often helpful to view several different translations to get a better flavor of the underlying meaning. In addition, the definition in your Webster's Dictionary might not be the same as the description in the original language. A Bible dictionary is an essential resource.

Exegesis versus Eisegesis

When I attended Fuller Theological Seminary, our professors constantly reminded us how critical it was to let the text divulge its meaning with the help of the Holy Spirit rather than interpreting it in light of our particular biases. Exegesis and eisegesis are the technical terms, respectively, for these two perspectives,[2] and they can be more subtle than one might think. I said in the introduction that my own knowledge of sin, salvation, and faith was largely shaped through the lens of the New Testament. This can be especially true for anyone trying to understand the initial chapters of Genesis because the information in those passages is so sparse.

Interpreting "The Fall"

John Calvin wrote "the whole third chapter of Romans is nothing but a description of original sin [vss. 1-20]."[3] The sin Calvin speaks of refers to Adam's transgression. Surely, we are on firm ground when we use one portion of Scripture to tell us what another passage means. After all, both are inspired by the Holy Spirit.

There is a problem with this logic, however. While it is true Romans and Genesis are inspired by God, we are actually using *our interpretation* of Romans 5:12-21 to enlighten our comprehension of Genesis chapter 3. To amplify what I mean, let's take a look at a few snippets from the passage in Romans.

> Therefore, just as <u>sin</u> came into the world through one man, and death through sin, and so death spread to all men because all sinned . . . Yet death reigned from Adam to Moses, even over those whose sinning was not like the <u>transgression</u> of Adam, . . . For if many died through one man's <u>trespass</u>, much more have the grace of God and the free gift by the grace of that one man Jesus Christ abounded

for many. . . . For as by the one man's <u>disobedience</u> the many were made sinners, so by the one man's obedience the many will be made righteous (Romans 5:12-19, *emphasis mine*).

Paul uses four words to describe Adam's action: *sin, transgression, trespass,* and *disobedience.*

Sin is the Greek term used to translate both the noun and verb forms of the Hebrew word in Genesis 4:7: "sin crouching at the door."[4] Its Hebrew verbal meaning can be "do wrong, commit a mistake or an error, miss the mark or miss the way"[5] —all depending on the context.

> *Paul uses four words to describe Adam's action:* sin, transgression, trespass, *and* disobedience.

This Greek moniker is an individual act[6] whose description closely follows the Hebrew definition. For Paul, it is not only a personal action but a plight which "embraces all humanity. The individual is always in this all-embracing state of sin."[7]

In general, *transgression* applies to sin in its relationship to the Law.[8] It does not necessarily imply a deliberate intent to violate the Law and can mean an overstepping which disobeys the Law.[9] For example, in 1 Timothy 2:14, Paul says Eve became a transgressor even though she was deceived by the serpent. Since she was deceived, violating God's command could not have been her premeditated purpose. Commentators Emerton and Cranfield, writing about the phrase *transgression of Adam,* say: ". . . it does not focus attention on the fact that Adam's sin was a transgression of a definite commandment, but rather characterizes it simply as a false step, a going astray . . . and so a misdeed which violated his relationship with God."[10]

Trespass indicates a wrong course of action, transgression, or sin most generally against God.[11] And *disobedience* means an unwillingness to hear.[12]

Rebellion is not mentioned in Paul's analysis of Adam's sin. Like the rest of us, you have transgressed against God's direct commands in the Law. But when you did, was your sin an act of willful rebellion against the Lord? That is, did you deliberately try to throw off His legal constraints to assert your own independence? Probably not. Whether your transgression was impulsive or done intentionally, it was likely a misstep—a going astray—or a falling short of the righteousness of God revealed in the Law. Since the consequences of Adam's transgression were so horrendous, some commentators, reflecting on his insubordination, have labeled it as rebellion. This analysis has happened repeatedly through the centuries.

In addition, all four words written by Paul portray an

event, and the only destructive effect of that occurrence was death. Because of this depiction and subsequent interpretations, Paul's revelation of sin as an adversary in Romans 6:12-14 and 7:8-24 is seen as a personification of sin—a literary tool utilized by Paul to help his readers better identify with the demonic aspect of sin. Little or no association is made between Romans 5:12-21 and his later passages or with Genesis chapter 4, where sin was originally defined.

Where did the use of Romans to interpret Adam's transgression lead the early Christian church? Let's review Romans 5:12-14 more thoroughly.

> Therefore, just as sin came into the world through one man, and death through sin, and so death spread to all men because all sinned—for sin indeed was in the world before the law was given, but sin is not counted where there is no law. Yet death reigned from Adam to Moses, even over those whose sinning was not like the transgression of Adam.

Paul says sin came into the world through one man, resulting in death that spread to all men from Adam to Moses because *all sinned*. Death prevailed even though their actions did not *count* as transgressions because they did not violate a particular command like the transgression of Adam.

Early Christian Scholars

So, how was the sin of the people living from Adam to Moses *counted* in a way that led to their death? Since Adam's original sin disobeyed a specific injunction, one solution proposed the condemnation for that one sin was counted not only against Adam but against all his progeny. That is, in Adam, all his descendants sinned. In this way, as stated by Romans 5:19, through the one man's disobedience, the many *were made* (passive verb) sinners.

According to early Christian scholars, original sin was passed on at conception as an inborn defect[13] of an individual's soul or spirit so that the person was not able to please God. This proposal faces two problems. First, little children would not be acceptable to the Lord. Yet Christ chose them as examples of those in the kingdom of God.[14]

The first boy born to Bathsheba and David[15] must also be acknowledged here. Bathsheba had been the wife of Uriah the Hittite and David had gotten her pregnant. David then had Uriah killed in battle so he could marry Bathsheba. But Nathan the prophet condemned David's actions and said the child would die. Even though David prayed and fasted, pleading for the child's life, the baby died after just seven days (circumcision takes place on the eighth day). When David learned the boy was dead, he said, "I shall go to him, but he will not return to me" (2 Samuel 12:1-23). David believed his uncircumcised son was with the Lord, and that he would one day join him.

> *According to early Christian scholars, original sin was passed on at conception as an inborn defect of an individual's soul or spirit so that the person was not able to please God.*

The second problem, even more consequential, is this: how could Jesus, a descendant of Adam, escape this defect of His Spirit? It was not taken away by circumcision because Elizabeth exclaimed upon seeing Mary, who was still pregnant, "And why is this granted to me that the mother of my Lord should come to me?" (Luke 1:43).

Calvin

Calvin and the reformers redefined the earlier solution. For them, the condemnation for original sin *removed* gifts and capabilities God had given Adam in the beginning. As a result, he was left naked and destitute. Further, his corrupted image was passed on to his offspring at conception so that in Adam, all were soiled and infected with the contagion of sin in God's sight.[16] Once again, this option must deal with little children and the birth of Jesus.[17]

A Contemporary Interpretation

A contemporary interpretation of the events in Genesis chapter 3 can be found in the *Theological Dictionary of the New Testament*, volume one, pages 279-286, written by Gottfield Quell, an Old Testament scholar, edited by Gerhard Kittel, and translated from German to English by Geoffrey Bromiley, one of my professors at Fuller Theological Seminary and my mentor for my doctoral thesis. (I knew him personally, and Bromiley was a truly humble Christian man.)

As its name implies, this monumental work is not a commentary but a thorough treatment of every New Testament word of religious or theological significance. The Greek word for *sin* in Romans 5:12 in its noun and verb forms, together with their derivations, is researched in pages 267-316 of this volume. The Greek translation of the Old Testament during the first century was the Septuagint. Both the Hebrew and the Greek translations were cited along with other sacred and secular references. So, this exposition covers the usage of these words in Judaism, Hellenism, and the New Testament.

It is within the context of the assessment of this Greek

word for sin that the so-called account of the Fall is explained. Quell's interpretation begins by acknowledging the author of Genesis does not use this word.

> In this connection it is <u>particularly instruc-</u> <u>tive</u> that in the story of the fall in Genesis, i.e., in the one great passage in the OT [Old Testament] which deals thematically with the religious problem of sin, <u>we do not find at all</u> <u>the customary terminology for sin</u>, unless we are to count the very general term for evil. What sin is, is indicated in other ways in this passage (*emphasis mine*).[18]

The explanation for this absence is found in another excerpt.

> It is <u>striking</u> that in this story of the so-called Fall <u>no use whatever is made of the usual</u> <u>technical terms</u> apart from the particularly difficult [the author inserted the word for evil here]. <u>Only from the matter itself do we know</u> <u>that the reference is to sin</u>. Because the author seeks to mediate a view and to describe precesses of a typical kind <u>he must set aside these</u> <u>terms</u>. Their pedagogic nature would be <u>out</u> <u>of place</u> in an attempt to observe and portray life rather than to give a theological presentation of the results. <u>The latter is left to the theo-</u> <u>logically inclined reader</u> (*emphasis mine*).[19]

Two important observations can be made at this point. First, the author declares it is particularly instructive and striking that the Genesis narrative does not contain any customary terminology for sin. His solution for this omission: theological language would be out of place in the context of his depiction.

However, if it was so critical for the Genesis author to observe and portray life in chapter 3 that he *set aside* the religious term for sin, why did he insert it in the observation and portrayal of life between Cain and his brother Abel in chapter 4?

Second, the sentences "Only from the matter itself do we know that the reference is to sin" and "The latter is left to the theologically inclined reader" imply the *reader* is interpreting this passage within the context of his or her theological biases. No matter how logical such an association may seem, it does not follow that the original author also embraced the identical explanation for his portrayal of these events.

> The presentation continues.

> Only the clever serpent perceives the dispro-portion between the seriousness of the con-sequences, i.e., death, and the triviality of the forbidden action. . . The loyal answer betrays as yet no trace of skepticism, **but it does re-veal a readiness for it, and the serpent goes on to entice her**, [Quell has highlighted these words] creating the opportunity resolutely to renounce her literal conception of the prohi-bition.

> Yet it is part of the imperishable greatness of the story that, in spite of its clear recognition of the grotesquely misguided nature of the desire to be as God, it does not regard this as outrageous or disgraceful, but acknowledges it with the painful gentleness of an expertus.

> Nevertheless, as this effect is attained, with needle-like certainty there is a probing of the religious kernel of the problem of sin which is

concealed from all conceptual thinking. This is found in the incontestable immanent right of the ungodly attitude of man in his hostility to God (*emphasis mine*).[20]

Quell acknowledges there is no trace of skepticism in the woman's response to the serpent and that the "religious kernel of the problem of sin is concealed from all conceptual thinking." So his assumption of her readiness for skepticism can only be based on her words, "neither shall you touch it."

If this phrase revealed an underlying discontent with God's restriction, then it could provide the basis for this assertion. But there is another plausible explanation for her words: her husband added them as an extra codicil to protect her from even going near the tree. He also implied they were part of the original warning to give them added weight. Human history is peppered with similar examples.

Quell says there is a clear recognition that the couple's nature to desire to be like God was grotesquely misguided. Still, he acknowledges the narrator does not regard this as outrageous or disgraceful. How could there be a *clear recognition* of the nature of the couple's desire if the text says so little that might support this contention?

It seems odd that in the midst of the bounty spread out before them in the garden, they chafed and grew hostile toward God because of His restriction to refrain from the fruit of this *one* tree. When questioned by the Lord, Adam's wife said she was deceived by the serpent. Her statement is *clear recognition* that she misunderstood the serpent's directives and that her mental posture was neither ungodly nor hostile.

As stated earlier, there is another reason Adam and his wife wanted to be like God. If your children want to be just like you when they grow up, their aspiration is not a grotesquely misguided expression of an antagonistic craving for independence from you because you have not given them everything they wanted—it is just the opposite. They are paying you one of the greatest compliments they can bestow. Adam and his mate were no different. They too wished to be more like their loving heavenly Father.

The presentation continues.

> The words: "They knew that they were naked," are in the style of the story a way of saying that the wrongdoers were <u>suddenly conscious of a feeling of insecurity</u>. This feeling the narrator thinks he can best interpret by the feeling of <u>shame</u>. At the same time he incidentally answers the question of the origin of this remarkable feeling by showing that it is a consequence of sin and very close to, although not identical to it. <u>Without sin the man and woman would have had nothing to hide from one another</u>. Because they transgressed, they lost their state even in the physical sphere. . . .

The more strongly, however, this interpretation is theologically emphasized, the more clearly it must be stated that the aim of the author is not to give a correct theological account, but rather, if we may use the phrase, to popularize a basic theological concept. . . . Hardly anywhere else in the OT do we encounter discussion of a religious question which is so penetrating and yet sustained by such piety (*emphasis mine*).[21]

This interpretation declares the consequence of sin produced a feeling of shame. Had the couple not sinned, they would have nothing to hide from each other. Even so, it seems odd their transgression of God's command would suddenly yield a sense of insecurity toward *one another*. Their feelings of shame and nakedness would seem more appropriate to their later encounter with God since it was His warning they disobeyed. Further, there is nowhere in this presentation an explanation of how their sin led to death *in the day they ate the forbidden fruit*.

The exposition of Genesis ends as it began: by emphasizing the aim of the narrator was not to give a correct theological account. Once again, this shows a reluctance to consider another interpretation might exist that would credit the narrator with an accurate theological assessment.

The entire treatment of sin ends with these summary conclusions.

We have seen (1) that sin is the reality which, with creatureliness, determines the nature of the world; (2) that essentially sin is the rejection of the claim of God by self-assertive man . . . ; and (3) that redemption is summed up in the remission of sins. This is what distinguishes the NT in relation to Hellenism and Judaism. This is the form in which the Christ event is known (*emphasis mine*).[22]

Quell's interpretation of Genesis chapter 3 is delineated within the larger context of a thorough description of one of the Greek words for sin. It also states that sin "is understood as an individual act."[23] So, it is not surprising at the conclusion of this treatise the authors would say "that redemption is summed up in the remission of *sins*." As I stressed earlier, if our perception of redemption is evaluated as being no more than the remission (the cancellation of a debt, charge, or penalty) of sins (a list of errant acts), then we have lost sight of the more profound aspect of salvation: namely its ability to deliver us from the underlying wellspring of sin—the knowledge of good and evil we inherited from Adam.

An Alternative Proposal

As an alternative solution, if we interpret sin through the lens of Genesis chapters 3 and 4, we see that Adam gained an intellectual aptitude because of his transgression of God's command: the knowledge of good and evil. With this newly acquired understanding, he compared his own individual differences with those of his wife, resulting in feelings of nakedness and the desire to clothe himself.

Of course, his makeshift garments were useless when he contrasted himself with the Lord, leading to separation not only from his mate but from God. Adam's transgression which took place "in the day" he ate the fruit linked this severance with death—relational and spiritual death.

The ramifications of relational death would condemn Adam, Eve, and their heirs to physical death because of the debilitating stress it would produce throughout their lives. Since they had not been created to cope with this kind of emotional strain, their bodies would incur destructive repercussions and they would return to the dust of the earth. Initially, this devastating process took hundreds of years because the Spirit of the Lord, abiding in them, counteracted the effects of stress with the fruit of the Spirit. But the human race became so corrupt the Lord said He would not always strive with mankind, and therefore the extent of their days would be one hundred and twenty years (Genesis 6:3).

> *The ramifications of relational death would condemn Adam, Eve, and their heirs to physical death because of the debilitating stress it would produce throughout their lives.*

This intellectual skill poisoned the relationship Cain had with his brother, prompting the Lord to say:

> "If you <u>do well</u>, will you not be accepted? And if you <u>do not do well</u>, sin is crouching at the door. Its desire is for you, but you must rule over it" (Genesis 4:7, *emphasis mine*).

The capacity to comprehend what it meant to "do well" or "not to do well" was now part of Cain's makeup. The Lord did not merely personify sin as an adversary crouching at the door so Cain could better grasp its significance. The knowledge of good and evil he inherited from his father colored every aspect of the situations he faced daily and even stoked his emotional hatred toward his brother.

God's admonition to "rule over it" meant Cain must overcome his humiliated feelings—that the Lord did not regard his sacrifice in the same way as Abel's offering—or sin crouching at the door would tempt him to do much worse. Instead of "ruling over it," Cain relied on his own understanding and decided the only way he could avenge his humiliation was to rise up against his brother and kill him: a sinful act prompted by the *wellspring of sin*—his knowledge of good and evil.

The apostle Paul wrestled unsuccessfully with this adversary, as we can read in Romans 7:7-25. Paul's knowledge of good and evil—his flesh—produced in him all kinds of covetousness because of the Law: "You shall not covet." How? When Paul compared his resources with his neighbor's assets, he felt naked in that he desired (coveted) to "clothe himself" in what they possessed. This fountainhead of sin deceived him into thinking he would be more able to measure up, to be more successful, more satisfied, or more sure of himself if only he could obtain what other people enjoyed.[24] Unfortunately, it separated him from them and from the Lord, creating the stress of relational death (Romans 7:7-11).

This alternative proposal does not require an inborn defect or the lack of gifts and capabilities to be passed down from Adam because it does not limit the concept of sin to wrongdoings such as the four mentioned in Romans 5:12-21. More precisely, it identifies the inherited resource as the intellectual capability Adam acquired as a consequence of his transgression.

Even though Jesus acquired this capacity from Adam, He was previously endowed with the knowledge of good and evil as the Son of God. So He was not tempted by it to do anything on His own authority.

Furthermore, even though little children inherit this potential from their parents, it is not developed enough to create feelings of nakedness. This is not to say they never disobey or try to assert their own will! Of course they do. But these actions do not cause them to perceive they are naked. Here is a brief example of what I mean.

* * * * *

Several years ago, my wife and I were in our backyard on a hot summer Sunday afternoon. We heard laughter and squealing: children's voices coming from our neighbor's backyard. We peered over the fence to see what the commotion was all about. Our neighbors were having a party and the parents were laughing at the antics of their two-year-old twin girls. As we watched, each girl in turn scampered headlong through the brisk spray of a lawn sprinkler while gleefully trying to out-shriek her bare naked sister.

The scene was indeed humorous. But I can assure you none of the onlooking adults, ourselves

included, would have stripped down to our birthday suits and participated in the frolicking with the
same unbridled innocent delight. The little girls had
no sense of nakedness even though they knew the
rest of us were laughing at them.

* * * * *

Why This Alternative Is Important

Why is a more comprehensive definition of sin significant as outlined in this alternative proposal? If we recognize
the root of sin is our mental capacity to discern good and evil,
then we can begin to understand we are *incapable* of overcoming this antagonist. As long as we try, we will be functioning
under the law of sin and death. But if we quit trying—if we die
to sin—and believe there is no condemnation for those who
are in Christ Jesus, then we can live according to the law of the
Spirit of Life and walk in the light as He is in the light.

This alternative changes the focus of the Gospel. If sin
is only characterized as transgressions, offenses, and disobedience, it can be perceived by non-Christians as a lifelong in-
ventory of errant acts and salvation as a sacrificial payment
for those infractions. As long as the list does not contain any

grievous sins, these persons are likely to view themselves as "good people," not "sinners," with little or no need to restore fellowship with God and be born again. If they do join a church, it is probably more for the fellowship with other good people than for the desire to be reconciled to God.

One only needs to listen to each day's news to recognize our world is in serious trouble. We are tempted to look to law enforcement, social services, and other government agencies to stem the tide of evil eating away at the core of our society. But Jesus said:

> "You are the salt of the earth, but if the salt has lost its taste, how shall its saltiness be restored? It is no longer good for anything except to be thrown out and trampled under people's feet" (Matthew 5:13, *emphasis mine*).

Salt accomplishes two things: it adds flavor to our food and is a preservative. In both instances, only a little salt is necessary—but only if the salt is pure.

We are the salt of the earth. If non-believers consider the Gospel is no longer relevant because of the way they see themselves, then our "salt" has lost its saltiness and cannot function as a flavor and preservative for our world. If their perception of sin is diminished to a litany of offenses, then the Holy Spirit's ability to convict the world of sin (John 16:8-10) so the Father can draw people to His Son Jesus Christ (John 6:44) is also limited.

Regaining a more thorough definition gives us the opportunity to point to the wellspring of sin—to the knowledge of good and evil—and ask: "Who told you that you need to be thinner, younger, healthier, prettier, more athletic, more intelligent, one who speaks with more confidence, or have a better sense of humor?; have a bigger home in a more upscale neighborhood, a more impressive job with a larger paycheck?; have a newer, faster, or classier car, more stylish clothing, influential friends, or more time to devote to the things you want to do? And why are you 'clothing' yourself with the trappings of wealth, education, a notable position, or even religious piety so you no longer feel vulnerable?"

We are the salt of the earth. If non-believers consider the Gospel is no longer relevant because of the way they see themselves, then our "salt" has lost its saltiness and cannot function as a flavor and preservative for our world. If their perception of sin is diminished to a litany of offenses, then the Holy Spirit's ability to convict the world of sin (John 16:8-10) so the Father can draw people to His Son Jesus Christ (John 6:44) is also limited.

Then, we can present the Gospel as God's remedy to save people from their futile attempts to be accepted and whole, and help them to be clothed in His righteousness through a personal relationship with Jesus Christ.

> *Who told you that you need to be thinner, younger, healthier, prettier, more athletic, more intelligent, one who speaks with more confidence, or have a better sense of humor?*

Follow Christ

All Christians are called to follow Christ and, as members of His body, to function as light and salt to the world. Jesus identified three things a person must do to follow Him.

> "If anyone would come after me, let him <u>deny himself</u> and <u>take up his cross</u> and <u>follow me</u>. For whoever would save his life will lose it, but whoever loses his life for my sake will find it. For what will it profit a man if he gains the whole world and forfeits his soul? Or what shall a man give in return for his soul?" (Matthew 16:24-26, *emphasis mine*).

Deny Your Self

The knowledge of good and evil is a ruthless taskmaster, and it is at the heart of your expression of self. Even if you clothe your *self* with everything the world can offer in an attempt to be complete and fulfilled, you will always find circumstances that undercut your confidence, leaving you feeling vulnerable and naked. The author of Ecclesiastes describes a life spent in such a pursuit.

> "Vanity of vanities," says the Preacher, "vanity of vanities! All is vanity. <u>What does man gain by all the toil at which he toils under the sun</u>?" (Ecclesiastes 1:2, 3, *emphasis mine*).

> *Even if you clothe your self with everything the world can offer in an attempt to be complete and fulfilled, you will always find circumstances that undercut your confidence, leaving you feeling vulnerable and naked.*

Take Up Your Cross

The Gospel will never be popular. During His final Passover feast with His disciples, Jesus warned them with these words.

> "If the world hates you, <u>know that it has hated me before it hated you</u>. If you were of the world, the world would love you as its own, but because you are not of the world, but I chose you out of the world, therefore <u>the world hates you</u>. Remember the word that I said to you: 'A servant is not greater than his master.' <u>If they persecuted me, they will also persecute you. If they kept my words, they will also keep yours</u>" (John 15:18-20, *emphasis mine*).

Don't be fooled into thinking there is some palatable way to share the Gospel so as not to be disliked, ridiculed, or persecuted. On the contrary, one of the hallmarks of committing your *self* to the lordship of Christ is that the world will turn against you. But note the last sentence: just as some gladly embraced Jesus' message, you will discover those who are receptive to your testimony as well.

Follow Me

Christ's relationship with his Father is a model for our relationship with Him. He said He could do *nothing* on his own accord, but only what He saw His Father doing (John 5:19). It might seem odd for Jesus to say there was one thing He couldn't do: accomplish anything by his own volition. After all, it is easy for us. Why should it have been impossible for Him?

Jesus revealed the reason in a conversation with Jewish detractors when He said, "I and the Father are one" (John 10:30). To do anything on His own authority would separate Him from His Father, bringing relational and spiritual death.

He denied His *self* and committed to the lordship of His Father, executing only what He saw His Father doing.

If you have been born again, the Father and Son came to dwell in you to sit on the throne of your life so you could be one with them and participate in Christ's relationship with His Father (John 17:20-23). The Father continues to love His Son and show Him all His works. And His Son continues to carry out what He sees His Father performing through you and the other members of His body, the church.

Jesus Christ is calling you to deny your *self*, take up your cross, and follow Him as He follows His Father. As you obey His call, He will continue to reveal His plan for you to be a light in this dark world, and to serve as salt to the earth.

My Favorite Doxology

Now to him who is able to keep you from stumbling and to present you blameless before the presence of his glory with great joy, to the only God, our Savior, through Jesus Christ our Lord, be glory, majesty, dominion, and authority, before all time and now and forever. Amen (Jude 24, 25).

Study Questions for Discussion

- If you were a translator, what would you do to make sure your version of the Bible accurately conveyed the underlying meaning of the original language?

  - Would you try to render every word and phrase as literally as possible or would you also try to make sure the *meaning* of the original text was conveyed in your edition as well?

  - If you lived in a country whose language did not contain any words for sheep or lambs, how would you translate Jesus as the Lamb of God?

    - Do you think there might be words in ancient Hebrew that are not in English? It is because of these and other circumstances that translation is not as straightforward as you might think.

- What is the difference between exegesis and eisegesis?

  - Why can't we trust that a passage in the New Testament will give us the correct interpretation of a passage in the Old Testament?

- Can you think of other passages in the Bible that might be misinterpreted because of eisegesis?

- In 1 Corinthians 13:12, Paul says that while we are on earth our comprehension of the truth is like seeing in a mirror dimly—it is only partial. In every age, sincere people of God have wrestled with the issues of their day and sought the Holy Spirit's guidance to "lead them into all truth" (John 16:13). From our perspective, their enlightenment may not seem complete. However, we are only able to see more clearly because we stand on their shoulders. Do you think it is because of the knowledge of good and evil we inherited from Adam that we tend to think our interpretation of the Bible is *right*? For example, do you feel you *know* which day of the week is the most appropriate to worship God, or how old the earth is, or what predestination means, or when Jesus Christ will return, or what is the correct way to baptize a person, or whether speaking in tongues is the best sign of being filled with the Holy Spirit? Micah 6:8 has always kept my understanding of the views of other sincere Christians in perspective.

- Does our insistence on a particular interpretation of the Bible unite believers or does it separate us, creating relational death in the body of Christ?
- Why is a more comprehensive definition of sin significant as outlined in my alternative proposal?
  - Does a more limited view of sin impede the Holy Spirit's ability to "convict the world of sin" (John16:8)?
    - Does the knowledge of good and evil contribute to a person's opinion of himself or herself as "good people?"
    - Our world is in serious trouble. Jesus said we are the salt of the earth. Does the state of the world say anything about the condition of our *salt*?
    - Why do so many non-believers perceive the Gospel as no longer relevant?
  - How does a more comprehensive understanding of sin enable us to point to the wellspring of a person's feelings of inadequacy—their knowledge of good and evil—and help them see that

they are incapable of *clothing* themselves so they no longer feel vulnerable?

- How can presenting the Gospel in this light enable us to show how God's remedy can clothe them in His righteousness through a personal relationship with Jesus Christ?

- Does God only call pastors, evangelists, and missionaries, or does He call all believers to function as part of the body of Christ?

  - What does it mean to deny your *self*?

  - What does it mean to take up your cross?

  - How is Jesus Christ our model when He calls us to follow Him?

  - God has chosen you to perform a unique role with His Son in the body of Christ. Will you heed His call to deny your self, take up your cross, and follow Him as light in this dark world, and serve as one who is salt to the earth?

Endnotes

Chapter One

1. The Hebrew definitions contained in this book were taken from:

    A. Francis Brown, S.R. Driver, and Charles A. Briggs. *A Hebrew and English Lexicon of the Old Testament* (Oxford: At the Clarendon Press, 1968).

    B. Points of grammar are taken from: E. Kautzsch, A.E. Cowley, eds. *Gesenius' Hebrew Grammar* (Oxford University Press, 1966).

Chapter Two

1. E. Ray Clendenen, Jeremy Royal Howard, eds. *Holman Illustrated Bible Commentary* (Nashville, Tennessee: B&H Publishing Group, 2015), 10. "If Adam added to God's command, he almost certainly had a good motive—after all, if Eve never touched the tree, she certainly would not eat its fruit."

2. I have included the unfortunate consequences of selecting fresh fig leaves for clothing since it underscores the desperation the couple must have felt to cover their nakedness and rid themselves of their

feelings of embarrassment. I know firsthand about the dangers of coming too close to the latex sap of fresh fig leaves. Many years ago, my wife and I visited my ninety-year-old grandmother in Phoenix, Arizona. My father's mother lived in a small home on a country lot, and in her backyard stood a towering fig tree. It was past its fruit-bearing prime, yet still produced many more figs than any individual or family could want. One afternoon, I retrieved a ladder and a bucket from her garage, climbed into the fig foliage, and began harvesting some of the best figs I have ever eaten. At first, I hardly noticed the redness on the back of my hands and upper arms. But by the time the bucket was full, I was spending more time scratching than picking fruit. I cannot imagine how uncomfortable it must have been wearing loincloths made from freshly picked fig leaves.

3. Genesis chapter 3 is not the only place in the Hebrew testament where a creature is given the ability to converse with a person. In this passage, Satan empowered the serpent to speak to Adam's wife. In Numbers 22:21-35, the Lord enabled Balaam's mule

to talk to the prophet.

4. The gender of the Hebrew word *offspring* or *seed* is masculine. So the emphatic pronoun in the last segment of Genesis 3:15 would be rendered as "he" to match this gender as long as "offspring" is interpreted to mean an individual descendant. On the other hand, it would be rendered as "they" if "offspring" is interpreted to denote the woman's extended progeny, which would include both male and female descendants.

5. Jewish Publication Society of America. *The Holy Scriptures According to the Masoretic Text* (Philadelphia, Pennsylvania, 1955). The Hebrew Bible I purchased as a graduate student at Fuller Theological Seminary translated this segment as "they shall bruise thy head, and thou shall bruise their heel." Two notes about this sentence: First, the word *heel* is singular in the Hebrew text and therefore is translated as a singular noun in the English edition. As an ancient language, a singular noun in Hebrew could at times be understood as plural depending on the context. Second, the bruising of the head has some-

times been interpreted to mean a mortal wound. However, the verb *bruise* does not carry that much weight particularly since "bruise your head" is likely ultimately directed at Satan, who remains very much alive today. The phrase more likely indicates that a much more debilitating injury would be inflicted on Satan than he would be able to impose.

6. You have heard the phrase "stress kills." Here are three of many URLs to back up this claim: http://www.livescience.com/2220-stress-deadly.html; http://www.mindbodygreen.com/0-14560/10-reasons-why-stress-is-the-most-dangerous-toxin-in-your-life.html; http://www.healthline.com/health-news/mental-eight-ways-stress-harms-your-health-082713#4. There are other factors contributing to a person's demise: various illnesses both pathogenic and genetic, exposure to environmental toxins, injury, poor diet, lifestyle habits, etc.

7. Since the husband is the head of his wife even as Christ is the head of the Church, the husband's relationship with his wife is meant to mirror their relationship with Christ. While Christ is the head of

the church, His relationship with us is in no way controlling or manipulative. Instead, His loving and supportive umbrella of protection, security, and sanctity enables us to blossom into our fullest potential—a posture the apostle Paul enjoins husbands to assume in their relationships with their wives.

8. http://www.sciencemag.org/news/2016/02/women-are-more-empathetic-men-yawning-study-suggests

9. 1 Corinthians 15:20–28; 42–49.

Chapter Three

1. See also Hebrews 11:4 for more evidence that the Lord set up an initial sacrificial system.

2. See Genesis 3:18–19 and 5:29.

3. J.A. Emerson, C.E.B. Canfield. *The International Critical Commentary on the Holy Scriptures of the Old and New Testaments, Romans* (Edinburgh: T. & T. Clark Limited, 1977), 370.

Chapter Four

1. I will begin this small sample list of commentators with a catalog of positions explicitly held by them so their positions can be referenced by letter after each entry in the list.

A. The phrase "neither shall you touch it" signifies a growing discontent or resentment with God's restriction not to eat the fruit.

1. Her entire response to the serpent was not a defense of God's authority but rather was spoken as an autonomous judge critical of His command.

2. The phrase was Adam's wife's idea.

B. The woman's analysis of the fruit is equated with 1 John 2:16.

C. The act of eating the fruit was a willful choice—a deliberate assertion of their desire to live independently from the Lord's authority as "gods knowing good and evil."

1. By eating the fruit, Adam plainly showed a contempt for the favors God had given them.

D. As a result of eating the fruit, Adam and his wife realized they were naked and their disobedience made them feel guilty.

1. Guilt produced shame, motivating them to clothe themselves.

E. Their disobedience was the real reason Adam

and his wife were afraid and hid from the Lord.

F. God's responded with judgment against His un-
faithful subjects. (There is little in the tenor of
these statements showing any redemptive aspects to God's pronouncements.)

G. In His mercy, God did not kill Adam and his wife
in the same day they disobeyed His command.

H. The serpent was actually the devil in the shape
and likeness of a serpent.

1. D. Guthrie, J.A. Motyer, A.M. Stibbs, D.J.
Wiseman, eds. *The New Bible Commentary:
Revised* (Grand Rapids, Michigan: Wm. B.
Eerdmans Publishing Co., 1971), 84-85.
Positions: A.1, C, E, F.

2. Charles T. Frisch. *The Layman's Bible Commentary, Volume 2, The Book of Genesis*
(Richmond, Virginia: John Knox Press,
1963), 14, 15, 31-34.
Positions: A, B, C, E, F.

3. Jon Courson. *Application Commentary, Old
Testament, Volume 1: Genesis—Job* (Nashville, Tennessee: Thomas Nelson, Inc., 2005),

10-14.

Positions: A.2, B, C.

4. Matthew Henry, Martin H. Manser, eds. *The New Matthew Henry Commentary* (Grand Rapids, Michigan: Zondervan, 2010), 9-14. Positions: C.1, D, D.1, E, F, H.

5. William MacDonald, Art Farmstead, eds. *Holman Illustrated Bible Commentary* (Nashville, Tennessee: Thomas Nelson Publishers, Inc., 1990), 35, 36. Position: B.

2. The phrase, "who was with her" implies that Adam was at least in the vicinity. However, since he did not mention the serpent in his reply to the Lord in Genesis 3:12, his response also seems to imply he was not close enough to her to hear the serpent's queries. My account at the end of chapter 1 says that Adam's wife left him and traveled *toward* the north end of the garden. Since the tree of the knowledge of good and evil was in the *middle* of the garden, she may have walked only a short distance before encountering the serpent. This would also help explain why Adam

was so surprised that his wife returned so quickly when her original intent was to harvest almonds.

3. John Baille, John T. McNeill, Henry P. Van Dusen, eds. *The Library of Christian Classics, Volume XX, Calvin: Institutes of the Christian Religion* (Philadelphia: The Westminster Press, 1967), 245. "Adam was denied the tree of the knowledge of good and evil to test his obedience and prove that he was willingly under God's command . . . served to prove and exercise his faith."

Chapter Five

1. Matthew 6:30, 8:26, 14:31, 16:8; and Luke 12:28. In Matthew 6:30, Jesus coined a single word, "oligopistoi" (a transliteration into English). "Oligos" is a Greek word meaning small, little, or short—we get the word oligarchy from it. "Pistis" is the Greek word for faith. The "oi" at the end makes the noun plural. Alfred Marshall translates this word as "little-faiths" to provide as literal an interpretation as possible. See Alfred Marshall. *The Interlinear Greek-English New Testament, 2nd Ed. The Nestle Greek Text with a Literal English Translation* (Grand Rapids, Michigan:

Zondervan Publishing House, 1958), 23.

2. William Sanford LaSor. *Daily Life in Bible Times.* (Cincinnati, Ohio: Standard Publishing, 1966), 35–38, 93–95.

3. Jesus Christ's Hebrew name was Joshua.

4. While the actual site for the Sermon on the Mount is uncertain, tradition places it on Mount Eremos, a hill just west of Capernaum. http://www.bibleplaces.com/mtbeatitudes/

5. Romans 4: 3, 9, 22, 23; Galatians 3:6; Genesis 15:6 is also found in James 2:23.

6. Francis Brown, S.R. Driver, Charles A. Briggs, eds. *A Hebrew and English Lexicon of the Old Testament* (Oxford University Press, 1968). According to this lexicon, these three words are first used in Genesis 15:6.

7. First use of the word *righteous* in the Hebrew Testament.

8. In Romans 4:1–5, Paul builds on Genesis 15:6 to underscore that righteousness was not awarded to Abram based on any work he did but solely on his belief in God's faithfulness.

9. There is another side to faith—how it molds our character.

> Count it all joy, my brothers, when you meet trials of various kinds, for you know that the testing of your faith produces steadfastness. And let steadfastness have its full effect, that you may be perfect and complete, lacking in nothing. If any of you lacks wisdom, let him ask God, who gives generously to all without reproach, and it will be given him. But let him ask in faith, with no doubting (James 1:2–6).

Several elements about this passage stand out. First of all, our normal posture when facing trails is *not* to "count them with all joy." So, James asks us to look past the trials to the knowledge that such testing produces steadfastness. This act of self-discipline will keep us from reacting emotionally to the situation and enable us to seek guidance from the Lord.

Second, trials are not a generic category. They are trials that test our *faith*. Since faith is a relationship, we can rest in the knowledge that God will not allow us to be tested beyond what we are able to bear. He will provide a way for us to overcome the trial/temptation (1 Corinthians 10:13).

Third, the goal of these trials is to produce a complete and balanced character.

Finally, in the midst of these trials of faith, we can ask for His wisdom and it will be given—unless we doubt that God is faithful and will lead us.

Trials also include suffering. See Acts 9:15, 16; 2 Corinthians 12:7–10; Philippians 3:10, 11; 2 Timothy 3:12; Hebrews 2:10.

10. See Mark 16:15–20.

Chapter Six

1. https://www.hymnary.org/text/amazing_grace_ how_sweet_the_sound

2. Gerhard Kittel, ed., Geoffrey W. Bromiley, translator into English. *The Theological Dictionary of the New Testament* (Grand Rapids, Michigan: Wm. B. Eerdmans Publishing Company, 1977), 3:318–323.

3. See also Hebrews 8:1-10:18 for another account of Christ's propitiation as the fulfillment of the Hebrew testament ritual.

4. I have underlined *we* in this verse from Galatians to underscore the fact that Paul, a Jew, included himself. Therefore *everyone* is now able to receive the promised Spirit through faith.

5. God is spirit, and He possesses the knowledge of

good and evil as a quality of His spiritual being. Initially, the Lord created Adam and his wife without this knowledge. But when they ate the fruit, they became as gods knowing good and evil. That is, because they were created in God's image and likeness, and because this knowledge was part of His spiritual being, it became part of their spiritual being as soon as Adam transgressed and ingested the fruit. We inherited this knowledge from Adam through our parents—spirit to spirit. It is not passed down genetically.

6. H.E. Dana, Julius R. Mantey, *A Manual Grammar of the Greek New Testament* (Toronto: The MacMillan Company, 1957), 157.

7. http://animals.mom.me/differences-between-chrysalis-cocoon-7964.html

8. There are two words for *repent* in the New Testament. One of them is rarely used and is found only in Matthew 21:30, 32, and Matthew 27:3; 2 Corinthians 7:8; and Hebrews 7:21. Its basic meaning is remorse for the given action and is usually translated as a *change of mind*. The root meaning of the more

common word is a *change of heart*. With the former, a person expresses regret for the consequences of his actions but this change of mind does not provide any lasting relief. That remedy is enabled by a change of heart. See Gerhard Kittel, ed., Geoffrey W. Bromiley, translator into English. *The Theological Dictionary of the New Testament* (Grand Rapids, Michigan: Wm. B. Eerdmans Publishing Company, 1977), 4:626–629.

9. The tense of the verb translated "reach" or "come to" indicates a specific point of time when the change of heart takes place, meaning God's desire is that everyone be born again. Unfortunately, not everyone wants to have a change of heart.

10. The reason for my lack of feeling that I belonged had little to do with the church family itself. Today, whenever my wife and I visit relatives in Palmer, we attend the Catholic church. It is filled with young families in multiple services, and is alive with the Spirit of Christ.

11. http://www.4laws.com/laws/englishkgp/default.htm

Chapter Seven

1. W.F. Arndt, F.W. Gingrich, eds. *A Greek-English Lexicon of the New Testament and Other Early Christian Literature* (The University of Chicago Press, 1971), 357.

2. Matthew 11:15, 13:9, 43; Mark 4:9, 23; Luke 8:8; 14:35; Revelation 2:7, 11, 17, 29; 3:6, 13, 22. Remember that we—as spirit beings—live in our physical body which is passing away (2 Corinthians 5:1, 2). Our physical ears are part of our physical body while the ears of our spirit are part of our spirit.

3. One might be tempted to place another restriction on God's voice: His message must be validated by some passage in the Bible. Simply put, if this were a criteria, what Scripture assured Noah that God wanted him to build the ark, or Abram to leave his father's land and travel to Canaan, or that his progeny would be countless as the stars?

4. W.F. Arndt, F.W. Gingrich, eds. *A Greek-English Lexicon of the New Testament and Other Early Christian Literature* (The University of Chicago Press, 1971), 875. This word means to guard, protect, or keep.

5. https://www.jewishvirtuallibrary.org/jsource/judaica/ejud_0002_0009_0_09260.html

6. http://www.catholicconvert.com/blog/2012/06/15/how-much-can-a-camel-drink/

7. A clarification: suffering is not a fourth way God leads us. It is in the crucible of suffering that God leads us. He does not initiate the suffering as an avenue to lead us.

Chapter Nine

1. J.D. Douglas, ed. *The New Bible Dictionary* (Grand Rapids, Michigan: Wm. B. Eerdmans Publishing Co., 1970), 481.

2. I encourage you to read Hebrews chapters 3 and 4.

3. This is the reason the Holy Spirit can declare to us the things that are to come (John 16:13).

4. Ephesians 4:11-16.

Chapter Ten

1. You also may be wondering why I have used so many biblical quotes instead of just referencing them in the text. There are two reasons: It has been my experience that most people—myself included!—do not often stop in the middle of a page to look up a

scriptural reference because it tends to break up the author's flow. I include the Scripture so the reader can actually see where my statements are coming from. In addition, here is what Isaiah says about God's Word:

> So shall my word be that goes out from my mouth; it shall not return to me empty; but it shall accomplish that which I purpose, and shall succeed in the thing for which I sent it (Isaiah 55:11).

2. https://en.wikipedia.org/wiki/Exegesis

   https://en.wikipedia.org/wiki/Eisegesis

3. John Baille, John T. McNeill, Henry P. Van Dusen, eds. *The Library of Christian Classics, Volume XX, Calvin: Institutes of the Christian Religion* (Philadelphia: The Westminster Press, 1967), 253.

4. Gerhard Kittel, ed., Geoffrey W. Bromiley, translator into English. *The Theological Dictionary of the New Testament*, 1:268, 294, 295.

5. Francis Brown, S.R. Driver, Charles A. Briggs, eds. *A Hebrew and English Lexicon of the Old Testament* (Oxford University Press, 1968), 306.

6. Gerhard Kittel, ed., Geoffrey W. Bromiley, translator into English. *The Theological Dictionary of the New*

Testament, 1:295.

7. Ibid, 309.

8. Ibid, 5:739.

9. W.F. Arndt, F.W. Gingrich, eds. *A Greek-English Lexicon of the New Testament and Other Early Christian Literature* (The University of Chicago Press, 1971), 617.

10. J.A. Emerson, C.E.B. Canfield, *The International Critical Commentary on the Holy Scriptures of the Old and New Testaments, Romans* (Edinburgh: T. & T. Clark Limited, 1977), 284.

11. W.F. Arndt, F.W. Gingrich, eds. *A Greek-English Lexicon of the New Testament and Other Early Christian Literature,* 627.

12. Ibid, 624.

13. John Baille, John T. McNeill, Henry P. Van Dusen, eds. *The Library of Christian Classics, Volume XX, Calvin: Institutes of the Christian Religion* (Philadelphia: The Westminster Press, 1967), 247.

14. Matthew 18:1-6, 19:13, 14; Mark 10:13, 14; Luke 18:15, 16.

15. 2 Samuel 11:1-12:23.

16. John Baille, John T. McNeill, Henry P. Van Dusen, eds. *The Library of Christian Classics, Volume XX, Calvin: Institutes of the Christian Religion*, 248-250.

17. I am not criticizing John Calvin or any other persons who have gone before us and have diligently pursued the truth. We all see in a mirror dimly and what we know is partial (1 Corinthians 13:12); no one has a complete picture of the truth. From Polycarp to Augustine and from Calvin and Luther to the present, we stand on the shoulders of faithful servants of Christ and are indebted to them for following the leading of the Holy Spirit.

18. Gerhard Kittel, ed., Geoffrey W. Bromiley, translator into English. *The Theological Dictionary of the New Testament*, 1:279.

19. Ibid, 281.

20. Ibid, 281-283.

21. Ibid, 284, 285.

22. Ibid, 316.

23. Ibid, 295.

24. These are hypothetical examples based on Paul's reference to "You shall not covet."

NOTES

................Retire Smart

Virginia F. David Cleary